About the author

Sullivan McLeod grew up with three brothers in Margaret River and still lives there (often in a tree house) when he's not travelling. He performed around the world as a stand-up comedian for seven years with gigs at Melbourne Comedy Festival, Edinburgh Festival, London Comedy Store, Improv Comedy Club (LA) and The Comedy Store (LA). Apart from being a restless vagabond, he has been a door-to-door salesman for a telecommunication company (Sydney), a spy for a Greek Restaurant (Rhodes), an assistant to a professor to check the originality of ideas (European Patent Office, Holland), a canvasser for dodgy solicitors to see if anyone wanted to sue their landlord (London), an audience member paid to laugh at lame jokes for live TV shows (Hollywood), a driver of a drilling rig without a truck driver's licence (Kalgoorlie), and a stooge for a magician in his street show in London. And he's been a professional surfer for nine months.

the true story of my probably insane quest to become a professional surfer

Tunnel Vision

Sullivan McLeod

ALLEN&UNWIN

To the loveable rogues that are my family (D, Shoogs, AJ, Snags and Frags)
Thanks for everything.

First published in 2009

Allen & Unwin
83 Alexander Street
Crows Nest NSW 2065
Australia
Phone: (61 2) 8425 0100
Fax: (61 2) 9906 2218
Email: info@allenandunwin.com
Web: www.allenandunwin.com

National Library of Australia
Cataloguing-in-Publication entry:
McLeod, Sullivan, 1976–
Tunnel vision : the true story of my probably insane quest
to become a professional surfer / Sullivan McLeod.
1st ed.
ISBN: 978 1 74175 713 2 (pbk.)
McLeod, Sullivan, 1976–
Surfers – Australia – Biography.
Surfing–Australia.
797.32092

Cover and text design by Design by Committee
Typesetting by Pauline Haas, Bluerinse Setting
Printed and bound in Australia by McPherson's Printing Group

1 3 5 7 9 10 8 6 4 2

Contents

The Decision

I decided to be a professional surfer a few years ago in a sauna in Norway. There is a dramatic story I often tell people about how I was drawn to living in a town in Norway but it's too long and complicated to tell now—let's just say it involved falling in love with a girl and eating magic mushrooms. In Norway, I was partying and drinking and trying to think up ways to make money because the place is ridiculously expensive. One day I met some Australians in the town and we borrowed surfboards and went to the beach, ran across the ice-capped dunes and spent three hours freezing our arses off. After the surf, we drank beer in a sauna and started doing that thing Australians do in another country, which is to be even more Australian.

'What are you going to do next year?' one of them asked me.

'I'm going to be a professional surfer,' I replied, then burped and added, 'by the way, chuck us another beer.'

I'd said it like that at the time to spark a laugh but subconsciously the thought was planted. A little seed that would grow and grow and never let go. Of course, the idea was completely ludicrous because to go on the pro surfing tour you need money and surfing ability and I had little of either. In a lifetime of silly ideas this was my silliest.

Two years later I found myself in London a week before Christmas with the pro surfing idea still rattling audaciously around in my head. In London, I knew I couldn't improve my surfing skill but had a plan to make money to fund the tour. I'd seen a poster in the city looking for 'fit males between the ages of 25–30 for drug tests'. It was a corny ad—four guys flashed Colgate smiles around a pool table—but it claimed you could make £3000 a test and because of that I decided to do it.

On the bus to the hospital there were twice as many people standing as sitting and no one looked happy. Most shared the same expression, unable to hide a loneliness that had crept up behind the flesh and settled in for winter. I'd lived in London before and recognised the look. One week before Christmas, it's the cultural heart of the world and the loneliest place on earth.

A girl with brown skin and brown eyes squeezed past me in the aisle of the bus and we traded eye contact. She was beautiful, but there was also weariness in her eyes—as if the city had strangled the energy from inside her. I had the urge to spark a conversation and lift her spirits and also I was attracted to her but instead I lamed out and decided to Google 'lonely in London' later. (One heading on the Lonely Planet books and two million on porn.)

At Liverpool Street, I disembarked the bus and walked in the direction of the drug-testing centre. There was no time to be nervous. Inside, I passed an envelope containing my health history to the receptionist. She looked up, smiled and told me to go through to the debriefing room.

The debriefing room was white and had that hospital smell. Around the room were guys my age. They were square-jawed and blue-eyed, I guessed Eastern European. We were all there for the cash. Three thousand pounds sounded good to me but, no doubt, even better to someone from Poland or Russia. I scoured the room—so far no sight of a pool table.

The doctor walked in. I guessed he was the kind who'd prefer to stroll in but those days were beyond him. He sat down with a sigh, glanced at a clipboard and said: 'Welcome everyone. I'm sure you're all feeling a little anxious so let's begin. We have everyone's physical and mental records and have classified you with the drug that we think will be best.'

And then he began a kind of roll call; first mentioning our names, then the disease to be tested.

'Laudaff?'

'Yes.'

'You'll be testing arthritis.'

'Okay.'

'Nothing much to be worried about. I'll go through it with you later. Rietsberg?'

'Yep.'

'You'll be testing drugs for high blood pressure.'

'Okay.'

'Should be fine. Not too many side-effects for that one.'

'McLeod?'

'Yes,' I replied, beginning to feel comfortable.

'You'll be testing schizophrenia.'

'What?'

'You'll be testing schizophrenia.'

I leant back in my chair and wondered if the hospital staff had already conspired against me. Why was I the only one testing drugs for nutters? One of the Eastern Europeans gave me a camaraderie wink. Bloody Eastern Europeans.

'Hey look,' the doctor said in boyish tones after the roll call, 'I can see why you fellows might be a little apprehensive but there's nothing to worry about. As a young medical student I even tested some of the drugs myself.'

With his frail gait and gaunt features, the last comment was not necessarily reassuring. I should have been worried by the doctor's casual approach but was actually starting to warm to his humour—the way he stood in the doorway after the safety speech, clapped his hands together and said, 'Right, first victim?'

We were each going to have a private consultation before the tests. One final chance to pull out. When it was my turn, I questioned the doctor about why they chose me to test schizophrenia.

'Surely you'd want someone already with the disease, that way you could see if the drug works?'

'Nah, we just want to see if it enters your bloodstream,' he replied flippantly, and motioned me towards the bed. As he poked the needle into my arm, I conjured up an image of all the surfing I'd be doing in clear water under blue sky.

A nurse entered the room.

'Doctor, are you testing for schizophrenia?'

'Yes.'

'Oh.'

She looked confused.

'We're not meant to be testing anyone with the new drug, remember?'

Silence occupied the room. The doctor glanced at me and tapped a pen on his clipboard.

'Better wait for clearance,' he muttered and retracted the needle from my arm.

I left quickly. They were all mental. I'd have to find another way to fund the surfing tour but decided not to worry about money until later. I needed to be fit. It was time to get serious about training. It was time to go home.

Margaret River, January–March

I'm in Australia and hitchhiking with a girl on a highway from Perth to my home town of Margaret River. I met the girl last night. She has come from Melbourne to visit my cousin but he has working commitments so, on the spur of the moment, she decides to travel with me. Her name is Nicole. She's blonde and happy-go-lucky and we make a good hitchhiking team.

At first I feel sceptical about the prospect of a lift. We're in a spot where cars travel too fast to stop. But then I have an idea; I hide behind a tree so it looks like only the girl is hitching and, sure enough, a car pulls over. It's an old man who I think is going to be one of those typical Aussies who talk about football and fishing. Initially he does, but then he gets deep into the problems with his family; his only son died a few years ago and he has recently split from his wife.

It's a strange ride. Normally you just make polite conversation when hitching but the man has a tear in his eye and Nicole is telling him everything will be okay. For a while I feel sad but then the selfish part of me winds down the window and breathes in the fresh air and stares out at the peppermint trees and basks in the warm sun and is happy to be back in Australia.

The old man drops us about 30 kilometres from Bunbury and then to make things more surreal we're picked up by a deaf man. Conversation is not needed as he enthusiastically motions with his hands about the weather and other drivers. The deaf man drops us just south of Bunbury and we're barely going again when another car pulls up.

This time it's a guy in his early thirties. He seems to have plenty of money; the car is a new four-wheel drive and there are two new surfboards in the back.

'Where ya headed?' he shouts with a grin.

'Down to Margaret River.'

We jump in. His name is Richard. He's a spritely type who has just come back from working on a remote mine out in the west. After discovering Nicole and I are only friends he sparks up even more and, although his original destination is a town 30 minutes away, he suggests a wine tour. I've forgotten about people from West Australia — how an impromptu idea by a complete stranger can come across so naturally.

Inside the first winery, an old man behind an oak counter

greets us with an indifferent look. We try the wine and make conversation with the man, who fakes interest and appears to be sizing us up. I decide not to pull out my trump card—that my mum's the manager of the local tourist bureau.

We leave for another winery. This time the cellar-door salesman is a blond surfie type who greets us warmly and appears happy for the company. He lines up the wine samples and we eagerly drain them. Then he lines them up again and this process continues until we're all feeling merry. While overlooking the long row of vines I'm overcome by a sense of strangeness; I've been away for two years and here I am drunk in a winery not even 20 minutes from home.

We jump back in the car and Richard suggests we go surfing, which seems silly now that we're all boozed but I agree because of it. The first spot we arrive at is a break 15 kilometres north of Margaret River called Gallows. Having surfed it before, I know it can be challenging depending on the conditions but today the waves are small and crumbly. Richard lends me a board and I excitedly run down to the water edge. It has been two years since my last surf and two months since I've eaten much that isn't deep-fried, so my hips are flabby and white. I jump into the water quickly, trying to hide my body. Of course, the only people out there are people I know.

'Sully, long time no see,' says an old friend, who I went to school with, smiling. Then he points at my stomach. 'When are ya due?'

For the surfers of Margaret River, putting on weight is regarded as a crime somewhere between armed robbery and assault.

I paddle for my first wave, a small left, rise to my feet too slowly and get promptly pitched over the falls. I swirl underwater and then hit the surface gasping for air. I've lost it. I really can't do it any more. But then I catch one, ride across and finish the wave. I surf for another hour and then walk up the beach with a pounding heart. I'm 10 kilos off being fit and a whole lifetime off being professional.

Richard and I change out of our wetsuits among the coastal scrub near the sand dunes. Nicole has stayed in the car and is into the second bottle of wine. She holds out a glass for me as I wrap myself in a towel.

'Drink?'

'No thanks.'

Richard drops Nicole and me at my parents' place. I am one of four boys. Ash, 27, is living in London and Jack, 31, is on the East Coast. The only one still living at home is 14-year-old Connor. I haven't seen my family for a year and, apart from Connor gaining a few inches, nothing has changed. There's still spindly purple wisteria outside the veranda, still the cricket bat leaning against an old tin used as a wicket, and still the unfruitful fruit trees. They are happy to see me. I've been in this position before—the honeymoon phase. I introduce them to Nicole and, over a beer, tell them my plan for the future. From past experience, I know it's unwise to move back home without one.

'I'm going to be a professional surfer,' I declare.

'But I'd have a better chance than you,' replies Connor. A comment that, however accurate, does not stop a punch in the arm.

'I reckon I'll go alright with a bit of practice,' I continue.

'Yeah, maybe 10 kilos ago.'

Another punch. Another laugh.

They aren't taking me seriously but it doesn't matter. Tomorrow I'm going to start yoga.

Professional surfing is run on a two-tiered system. The World Championship Tour (WCT) is the pinnacle of pro surfing. Surf magazines refer to it as the 'dream tour'. On the WCT, there are only 11 events each year and they are held in exotic surf spots—from Kirra on the Gold Coast, to Jeffreys Bay in South Africa, to Pipeline in Hawaii. Only the top 45 surfers in the world can compete on it and at the end of the year a world champion is crowned. These events are backed by thousands of sponsorship dollars from rich surf companies and are beamed to millions around the world via the internet.

To make it onto the WCT you first need to start on the World Qualifying Series (WQS). This is the tour you go on if you ever dreamed of being a pro. There are still thousands of dollars in prize money on the WQS and the events are covered on the internet, but it's not as glamorous as the WCT. If the WCT is the major league of professional surfing, then the WQS is the minor. If the WCT is the blue ribbon 100-metre event, then the WQS is the gruelling marathon. If the WCT is the cream on the cherry, then the WQS is the sponge cake served to the side.

Although the majority of people on the WQS hail from prominent surfing countries like Australia, Hawaii, Brazil and America, there are also surfers from Spain, Mexico, and even Canada and Norway. On the WQS there are about 50 events each year — most in crumbling beach breaks. The competitions range in size, prize money and ratings points allocated from one star to six (1-star events have the least prize money and ratings points allocated to competitors and 6-star events have the most).

In WQS competitions there are four people in each heat and the top two surfers advance to the next round. Surfers are seeded in each WQS event according to points they've accrued from the previous year. Usually, the top-ranked surfers do not have to surf until the third or fourth round.

The heats are 20 minutes long and only your best two rides count. After you ride a wave, you are given a score out of 10 by five judges. Then the top and bottom scores from the judges are dropped, and the other three are averaged out, which leaves you with your actual score. Because only your two highest rides count in each heat, effectively, you're left with a score out of 20. I'm still not quite sure of the exact judging criteria for waves ridden in WQS competitions but, reading from the Association of Surfing

Professionals (ASP) website, it states that surfers will score well if they perform radical manoeuvres in the most critical section of the wave with speed, power and flow.

The goal of the WQS is to finish at the end of the year ranked in the top 15 places to qualify for the World Championship Tour. Making the top 15 is the dream. This is what draws hundreds of surfers to trawl around the world, continually haggling with airport staff to avoid fees for their boards. This is why they drag their surfing gear along the narrow streets of congested cities. If the contest's on, they'll happily surf on reefs where leaving with only one infected wound is counted as a lucky break.

Considering that most beaches in Australia, Hawaii and California (not to mention Brazil and Europe) have their share of talented surfers keen to try the WQS, it's incredibly difficult to qualify for the 'dream tour'. In 2005 there were 800 surfers ranked on the WQS; only 15 made it to the WCT. Needless to say, anyone who qualifies is a bloody good surfer.

I figure I'll spend eight months on the WQS, competing against the brash Aussies, the hard Hawaiians and the gung-ho Brazilians. Having made a few quick phone calls, I know I'll need to pay $15000 to the ASP and register myself as a WQS competitor before even entering an event, but my first priority is fitness. The plan is to spend some time training in Margaret River.

*

Margaret River is a funny sort of a town. Being primarily involved in tourism and only a three-hour drive south of Perth, the population can swell from 10 000 in winter to 20 000 in summer. There is one main street. There are builders and carpenters and electricians. There is a primary and a secondary school, more than 50 vineyards and a few famous wineries. The weather is cold and blustery in winter, hot in summer, cool in spring and beautiful in autumn. There is a river, which the town is named after, that runs out into a river mouth. There is a stretch of 30 kilometres of beaches and some of the best waves in the world.

Growing up, I was under the impression that the town was normal. Then I went travelling and realised that in other places you do not wag school and go to the beach, only to find that the teachers are already there. You do not happily employ tradesmen who down all tools at the hint of a new swell. If you are male, under the age of 30 and do not surf, you are not considered a freak. When someone starts a conversation with 'How was it?' you do not automatically assume they're referring to the waves.

In school, being a good surfer was the key to girls, drugs, parties and happiness. The only thing I wanted was to surf well. I can surf. I have been known to do the odd good cutback and the odd good re-entry and even get the odd tube, but I know I have never been a really good surfer. I have never crouched low and gracefully on bottom-turns, raced off the top and cracked it. I have never taken off behind a pitching lip and simultaneously pulled into the wave, and I still can't do those goddamn silly 360s. Kook is the name given by the surfing community to people who don't surf well and regardless of how hard I tried, I still spent my first few years surfing like one.

I blame genetics. My legs are too long and my hips are too wide. Of course, it's not just looking like a chiselled ironman that's important. Having harboured such a searing desire to surf well, I've often analysed what it is exactly that makes a good surfer. While learning, as I've spluttered for air in the ocean, I've watched good surfers push the nose of their board down with their knee to casually duck-dive an impending wave. When we make it to the breaking zone and a wave surges towards us, I've watched in wonder as they've turned, paddled, sprung to their feet and gracefully dropped down the moving crest of water. After I catch a wave and paddle back out, I've watched them come hurtling towards me, their board rocketing towards the top of the wave, and then in one fluid motion they'll twist and plumes of spray will be sent from the rail of their board skyward. Like anybody who's good at their sport, the good surfers make it look easy.

Learning to surf is not easy. Even the initial stages of duck-diving and riding a wave took me at least a year to grasp. In principle it sounds easy—the wave arrives, you paddle your board and then, when you feel it pick you up, you jump to your feet and ride it. I remember the first time I attempted to surf. I was about 11. My brothers and

I found some old surfboards that had graciously been left under a tree house by the previous residents. We took them down to the river mouth and I spent a frustrating hour being battered by the merciless ocean. The waves were only small that day and breaking on a sandbar 30 metres off the beach, but already I was hooked.

Back at home, my brother and I bashed the fins out of an old board and laid it on the dirt beside the house. We would attempt jumping from our stomach to our feet as quickly as possible. The practice of these bare mechanics of surfing did not speed up the learning curve much. Possibly, even as an 11-year-old, I should have known that it isn't just the transition of jumping from your stomach to your feet that's important. There is a combination of skills required. You need to be flexible, you need to be fit, you need to have the right surfboard, but most importantly you need knowledge of the ocean, and this can only be acquired from time spent in the waves. After a while, when looking at the shape of an approaching wave, you can sense if it will dump viciously or spill gently across the sandbar. On the paddle out you learn to go with the channel, which will deposit you safely out the back, instead of being stuck continuously fighting the breaking whitewater. You learn to relax your body when falling off a wave, instead of struggling against it. These little revelations came to me slowly but I was determined to learn, and gradually I became a strong swimmer and competent surfer.

Now that I'm in training, I'll need the kind of discipline

that's been absent for 29 years. The parties will have to stop. The blurry nights at Settlers Tavern will have to stop. I'll exercise every day. I'll spend a whole summer surfing every day, running every day, doing yoga every day and eating mostly fruit. This is it. Now or never.

I've moved into the tree house—the one I played in as a kid. I've equipped it with a double bed and desk and it's not a bad little sanctuary away from the house. Nicole spends three days enjoying Margaret River and then heads back to Perth. I'll miss her; she is open-minded and perpetually smiley.

One afternoon I go to a local sports store to speak to James Clark, an organiser of a WQS contest in Margaret River, who I hope will give me information on how to register for the Margaret River competition and the WQS tour. Clarky (all men in Australia must have a nickname) is strangely not too surprised at my questions. Too embarrassed to let him know I'm a serious competitor, I lie and tell him I want to be in the competition to write an article for a men's magazine.

'Oh yeah, which magazine are you writing for?' he asks, placing a fishing rod back in the rack.

'Um, can't tell ya, it'd be a breach of confidentiality.'

A co-worker, Anthony Bostok (nicknamed Ant or Boss depending on which name you prefer to shorten), comes bounding into the shop.

'G'day mate, you joining the pro surfing tour?'

'Nah, well, yeah, maybe.'

'Good stuff bro. Tell ya what, do ya want to come and play some underwater hockey with us tomorrow? It'll keep ya fit.'

Eager to lose weight, I agree and arrange to meet him the next day.

There are several reasons why I should have said no. One, because underwater hockey is a game as silly as it sounds. Two, because it's suggested by Anthony Bostok. And three, because Ant was given the idea by somebody from Tasmania.

A word on Ant: He's the uninitiated leader of a group of crazed free-divers living in the town. Three years ago, I was fishing with some friends about 2 kilometres offshore in a little dinghy. We were just about to throw in a line when we saw a float and a trail of fish bleeding and flapping around on the surface.

'What the heck is that?' I asked a friend.

'Oh, probably Ant. He must be doing a bit of snorkelling.'

I peered down but couldn't see him.

'Does he have an air tank down there or something?'

'Nah, just free-diving.'

Just then Ant came splashing to the surface with a fish on the end of a rusty old spear.

'G'day fellas,' he said. 'Comin' in?'

It'd been a bad summer for shark sightings. There

were constant front-page stories in the local paper about banning commercial crayfish boats from surfing beaches. The argument (a valid one) was that the meat used as bait in their pots was luring in sharks. There was a story drifting around town about a great white that had actually leapt out of the water at a popular swimming spot and beached itself. Sightings of reef sharks in the surfing areas were so common that one was actually nicknamed Bruce. Yet there was Ant, all alone, 2 kilometres out to sea, swimming around with bloodied fish trailing behind him and using a flimsy-looking spear as protection. I made up my mind then that the boy was nuts.

Tasmania, down at the bottom of Australia, is an island that draws the type of people who tend to have a beard. While travelling I discovered that a good part of the world views Australians like a drunk uncle at a wedding—harmless but good as a target of jokes. To counteract, Australians give the same treatment to Tasmanians. But here's the problem: Until people settle in Antarctica, there's really no other place for Tasmanians to laugh at. This makes them a resilient lot, and quirky enough to invent a game like underwater hockey.

A young Tasmanian traveller told Ant about underwater hockey. Apparently, Tasmanian divers play it to build oxygen capacity. I show up the next day at the local swimming pool and greet Ant and ten other muscly types. Ant lets me in on the history of the game. Initially it was a social event; the rules were loose, there was little physical contact and nobody really kept the score. But then, as will often happen when people from Margaret River get together, the games became competitive. There were teams and positions and umpires. Proper goals were made. Proper equipment was used. A rulebook in Tasmania was photocopied and sent over. They even began an annual competition against the Tasmanians — the National Underwater Hockey Championship. Of course, sometimes it's hard to have a national competition when 99 per cent of the nation doesn't know it exists. Undeterred by lack of mainstream recognition, the Margaret River boys, as I'm about to discover, play with a zest not dissimilar to cavemen hunting for wildebeests.

The rules of underwater hockey are as follows: Two teams of five swim around the bottom of a pool using miniature-sized hockey sticks to pass a puck. The object is to get the puck into the goal. When you need a breath you come to the surface, then go back down to continue the game.

I'm aligned to a team and, for some reason, they make me goalie. I quickly realise why it's the worst position; every time a goal is scored it's my responsibility. This is the conundrum: Get air and survive or stay below, stop the goal and pass out. After 20 minutes of making these crazy decisions I stay under for one extended piece of play and feel a buzzing in my leg. (My brother Ash, after suffering a horrific surf wipe-out, once described a similar experience. Apparently it's the body's way of convulsing before loss of consciousness.)

I surface and suck in deep breaths. With my legs still tingling, I drag myself up to the side of the pool, breathing hard.

'Something wrong?' suggests Ant, swimming up beside me.

'Just dying from lack of oxygen,' I almost say, but instead complain of cramp.

Ant offers a slightly agitated look, the kind given when a falling piece of toast lands face down.

'Oh well, I guess we'll have to play five on four.'

'I guess so,' I reply, and make up my mind to never play underwater hockey again.

My surfboard situation is dire. Here are the options presented from underneath the tree house. There's a long narrow single fin that has been shaped in the 1970s and is covered with a drawing of a snake. We call it the 'snake board'. My cousin's 6' 4" thruster, which is in good condition; however, I've been told not to use it. A kite board nicknamed 'the stonker' which, in our family, gets used as a surfboard. It's yellow and thick and made out of hard plastic with the strangest fins (normally surfboards have three fins but this one has five small fins running underneath the rails).

A pattern is formed: Use the stonker most of the time or my cousin's board if no one's looking.

Renata, a German girl I met in Indonesia two years ago,

has come to visit me. She's been travelling around Australia for six months and is in Margaret River for a week. She's 5'6", blonde, petite, and interested in learning to surf. Initially I feel ashamed about living in a tree house but she regards it as a novelty. Funny, these travelling European girls.

One morning we go surfing at the river mouth, a crumbly beach break where I first learnt to surf. After a few minutes she gets cold and goes in but I stay out, trying to impress her. When I come in she's sitting beside another guy. I walk towards them, feeling jealousy brewing.

'G'day mate, get any good ones?' the guy asks.

'Nah, there's not many out there.'

The guy is wearing shorts embroidered with the Australian flag and drinking a beer. His hair is blond and matted and his face carries a smile. I know him.

'Bloody hell Pizza Shop, long time no see,' I say.

'I thought you didn't recognise me,' he replies, holding his hand over his heart to fake being hurt.

'What have you been up to?' I ask, then listen as Pizza Shop (nicknamed so because he used to work in one) explains his story animatedly; he has four kids and has recently split from his wife. I've grown up around Pizza Shop but haven't seen him for ten years and detect a kind of madness in his eyes. Little did I know then that if 'going off the rails' is a term used to describe temporary insanity, then Pizza Shop has gone off the rails, over the creek, through the forest and joined a travelling circus.

I hang out with Renata for the week. I can't complain;

we spend the days surfing and the nights in the tree house. On Friday afternoon I drive into town to drop her at the bus going back to Perth. After discovering the bus isn't leaving for an hour, we walk to the pub.

Pizza Shop is in the beer garden.

'Look out, here's trouble,' he proclaims, as we sit beside him.

'Been busy?' I ask.

'Just got out of court. Check this out. The bureaucrats, in their infinite wisdom, have added this clause to reckless driving where you tell them you haven't had time to build a case and they'll postpone your hearing. It's awesome mate—I was meant to lose my licence months ago.'

When Renata tells him she's catching a bus to Perth, he says: 'Bugger that, I'll take you up. I was planning on going up there anyway. You should come with us Sully, we'll make a weekend of it.'

'Thanks, but I'm really broke at the moment.'

'No worries, I'll lend you money.'

I think about the prospect. There are a hundred reasons why I should say no but we jump in his car, a hotted-up Holden, and head off to Perth.

'Just need to make a quick pit stop,' Pizza Shop informs us, and pulls into a drive-through bottle shop.

'Half a carton of Coopers mate,' he shouts, head out the window.

We roll out of Margaret River with the sun setting, an Aussie rap tune blasting and Pizza Shop twisting his bottle top off with his teeth while driving one-handed. With Pizza Shop at the wheel, we make it to Perth in quick time. After dropping Renata off at the airport (she seems relieved to be alive) we make plans for the night.

'Better off starting in Northbridge I reckon,' Pizza Shop announces.

I enter the first place, the Aberdeen, feeling anxious. It's a pub with a reputation.

'Let's take it easy over here,' I tell Pizza Shop.

He's wearing a bright green T-shirt and a mad expression.

'No worries mate,' he says, giving me a playful punch on the arm.

I spend the night trying to protect him from fights. We leave in a drunken mess and sleep at a hostel in the city. In the morning I wake to the sound of yelling.

'Get up sleeping beauty.'

A six-pack of beer lands on the bed.

'Gotta love city licensing.'

We drive to the beach and drink all day. At night we stumble into a beachside pub with a live band. Inside, I scope the room and feel more comfortable; we're with our own—the dance floor is a mop of blonde surfie hair. This doesn't deter Pizza Shop, however, and within 20 minutes security demands that we leave, so we go down to the beach and pass out on the sand.

'Feeling pretty rough this morning,' Pizza Shop declares the next day. 'Better get some beers before the hangover kicks in.'

After squashing my protests he begins drinking again. This time we make plans for the Sunday session at the Cottesloe Hotel. The Cot is a beachside pub with a huge beer garden that's an institution for city folk on Sundays. Inside, Pizza Shop feeds me one of his antidepressants and things get blurry. It's the good kind of blurry, where you forget your worries and wander in a dream-like state. When the pub closes I lose Pizza Shop among the masses. I find him in his car, clutching his mobile phone with tears streaming down his face.

'She's a bitch mate.'

'What's wrong?'

'My wife, she's not letting me see my kids.'

He seems in a more manic state than usual and, moments after a patrolling police car drives by, he slides his car around the car park in an emotional rage. A group of people pull up beside us and cheer him on.

'What the hell are you doing?' I ask him, as the car slows and the smoke settles.

'Just having a bit of fun,' he says, his eyes revealing a mixture of raw wildness, antidepressants, emotion and alcohol.

Later, two girls ask us for a lift to another suburb. They squeeze in the car and, of course, Pizza Shop goes like a rally driver through the city. The girls laugh and will him on. When we arrive, we ask them if we can stay but they live with their parents so with no hotel booked, we decide to drive back to Margaret River.

Halfway there, while driving along the deserted highway, Pizza Shop falls asleep.

'Oi,' I yell, and grab frantically for the wheel.

'What the hell are ya doin'?' he snaps, waking abruptly.

'Pull over Pizza Shop, you're pissed.'

He refuses to stop and denies falling asleep, claiming it's a prank to see if I'm paying attention. After continual haggling, he stops driving and I take over.

In Bunbury we stop at a 24-hour petrol station and hear a waft of music coming from across the road. Concluding that there must be a nearby party, we stumble through the bushes, both high on alcohol and antidepressants. We walk around in the scrub for half an hour but find no sign of life in the darkness. Eventually we trek back to the car and discover the noise is actually music from inside the petrol station. We laugh at our silliness and approach the counter. No doubt spooked by our drunk and grubby states, the attendant refuses to serve us, so we swear at him and continue driving. At four in the morning we roll into Margaret River on the last drops of petrol. I crash on Pizza Shop's couch feeling empty; it has been a three-day bender. I'll start yoga tomorrow.

I'm nursing a vicious hangover on my parents' veranda and analysing the real reason behind doing the pro surfing tour. It seems to me that young Australians have never had it so good. There's only one thing better than being in the 'feel good' generation and that's being raised by them. We are healthy. We are educated. We have casual jobs that can be left and taken back on a whim. In our spare time we enjoy creativity, art and overusing words like surreal, random and abstract.

With all this security, the one thing that we crave most is insecurity. We want to live dangerously. We want to travel. We want to hike barefoot through Indonesian shanty towns and retell the story over a pint at our local. Soon, the stories themselves serve as tokens in a game of one-upmanship. It's not enough to have a bee fly under your helmet while on a motorbike. You need a whole swarm of bees trapped under your helmet, causing you to skittle across the road while narrowly avoiding the motorbike which has imploded in flames. It's not enough to consider studying Eastern philosophies. It's not enough even to have met the Dalai Lama. Eyebrows will be raised when you've met the Dalai Lama on an isolated mountain top near the Himalayas, he's invited you back to his spiritual temple in Tibet and you've stayed there for six months as his own personal gardener.

And the truth is, as far as exaggerated stories to entertain go, I've been the worst offender. I've travelled non-stop for seven years. I've been homeless in America, performed stand-up comedy in Edinburgh, and been chased out of Greece when caught working as a spy for a restaurant. At pubs, I've lapped up any laughter from the well-rehearsed tales like it's fuel for my soul.

And now how I wish this journey into pro surfing is just another irreverent story. How easy it would be to justify to myself that the reason behind it is to gain another whimsical anecdote to add to the collection. And this one has potential to get more laughs; I spend a year on a pro surfing tour. I drink. I party. I hardly make it on time for the competitions. I crack jokes at the other competitors to freak them out. I barely take it seriously at all.

But a few small incidents make me rethink the strategy. About five years ago, I was approached in the Margaret River Hotel by an older local.

'Bloody hell Sully,' he said, slapping me on the back and sizing me up with what appeared to be nostalgia, 'you've got bigger.'

'I can remember you surfing the point as a grommet,' he continued. 'You and Chris Ross were the only two young guys that could surf it. There was no one else your age with the balls.'

Although his comments were flattering, I thought they were misdirected. The normal cycle for surfers in Margaret River is to start at the forgiving river mouth and work your way up to the point. The point (or main break, as locals call it) is the most well-known wave in Margaret River. Because it breaks on a reef 300 metres offshore and picks up any fronts off the Indian Ocean, it has the potential for huge surf. I did surf the point as a teenager but spent most of the time floundering around in the whitewater. I was also amazed he'd put me in the same bracket as Chris

Ross, a freakishly talented local surfer who'd probably perform okay on the WQS.

And then a week ago, while walking up the stairs of the point after a surf, I spotted a friend I hadn't seen for years.

'G'day,' Paul said. 'Ant tells me you're doing the WQS this year.'

'Yeah, just doing it for a muck-around,' I replied quickly, secretly annoyed at Ant for spreading the news.

'I reckon you'll go alright,' Paul said.

I glanced at his face for a hint of laughter or mockery but his expression was deadpan.

'Really? You seriously think I'll go alright on the WQS surf tour?' I confirmed, just to be sure he understood the situation.

'Yeah mate, you might surprise yourself. I've always liked your style of surfing.'

I laughed off his compliments but went home feeling flattered.

These conversations have confirmed a feeling deep inside that's been trying to prise its way out. It's a feeling that should be repressed but it's down there somewhere, threatening to surface. And the truth behind going on the WQS is this: I think I've got a chance. I might even, in the right conditions and with a lot of luck, be able to beat some of the pros. Maybe, after years of practice, I've become a better surfer than I think. At worst I can test myself to find out how far I'm off their level.

But first, I not only need to improve my surfing; I need to find money. Anyone can register as an international WQS competitor but you need to pay $1500 to the ASP. An idea sprouts when my brother, Jack, comes to visit from the East Coast. He wants a bank loan for a helicopter pilot's licence and I convince him to extend it to fund my tour. Of course, Mum and Dad think we're both mental and a typical family row sparks. We apply for the loan ($60 000 for him and $20 000 for me) and two weeks later it's approved. (Proof the Australian banks will lend money to anyone.)

On the day of the loan approval I rock up at Pizza Shop's house with a bottle of wine, giddy with excitement. I've forgiven him for driving like a lunatic back from Perth and tell him about the WQS plan.

'Bloody hell, I'll go on the surfing tour with ya, mate,' he responds with enthusiasm.

The suggestion isn't as crazy as it sounds; I've surfed with him recently and been surprised by his ability. Excited at the prospect, we search the ASP website in a frenzy and pencil in possible events. There are WQS competitions in Australia in the near future but entry forms are needed a month in advance and we're too late. We decide to make our first competition the Mr Price Pro, which is held in South Africa in June. To celebrate, we head for the pub.

The competitors have arrived for the Margaret River Masters (the WQS competition held each year in March).

It's funny how it works; all of sudden they're in your little town, cruising up the main street with stealth-looking board bags mushrooming from the roof of hire cars. They lurk around the main surf spots and draw a swag of photographers. I'm too late to enter the competition but look forward to surfing beside them to see how my ability will compare.

I drive down to Gas Bay and paddle out to the surf. Gas is a sucky wave that throws over a shallow reef. There are four cameramen on the beach and one bobbing around in the water. In the surf, the pros all chat and laugh among themselves, exuding confidence. For the first 15 minutes I sit to the side of the break. It's an amazing spectacle from up close. They tackle the waves without fear and remind me of how beautiful surfing can be. When paddling for a wave, their eyes are not focused on the downward drop but 50 metres along the line of the wave. After making the drop, they pull hard up into the wave, being engulfed into the tunnel. The real beauty of watching this type of surfing up close is the tunnel riding. Their tunnel riding, where you surf the inside of the wave, is instinctive, fast and incredibly casual. After weaving through the tubes, I watch them kick off the back of each wave with speed and wonder if it's all part of a magic trick. How can they be so graceful and fast? I surf for a few hours catching some smaller waves but mainly feeling like a goose and trying to stay out of their way. On my way up the beach, I feel inspired but downhearted, knowing I'll never be that good.

A surfing legend, Mark Occhilupo, wins the competition controversially by gaining a last-minute interference call against another surfer. When Occy collides with another surfer, Jake Paterson, on a wave, the judges deem that Paterson has interfered and thus his highest score is halved. (I don't know how the judges have come to this conclusion. Watching from the beach, my initial thought is that Occy should be penalised.)

When the competition ends I stop by Pizza Shop's house and we go to the local pub. All night I watch girls chat up the professional surfers but I don't stand a chance—the local girls know me and, after two hours at the bar, I've morphed into a bumbling fool.

Pizza Shop starts the night in a happy mood and ends it by tackling a policeman. Outside the pub, mobs of angry police attempt to throw him in the back of a police car. People shout at the police and rally behind Pizza Shop. This is hardly surprising. In Margaret River, credibility is gained by being drunk or putting yourself in danger. Some people can do one of these well, others both, but not many do both at the same time. In the end, the police win and haul Pizza Shop back to the station.

When the pub closes I stumble back to Pizza Shop's house and fall asleep on his couch. I wake in the night to a piercing scream.

'Faaaarrrrrkkkkk.'

Heading towards the noise, I discover Pizza Shop on the floor, dragging himself towards the toilet.

'What happened?'

'The fuckin' cops took out my knee.'

In the morning we get a knock on the door. It's the police. Pizza Shop is summoned to appear in court, charged with assaulting an officer. We sip coffee and discuss the consequences. The court case is not for two months, so he'll be unable to do the tour. He apologises for letting me down but I don't mind. Deep down, I always knew he was never going to make it.

I go home and form a plan. The loan has come through but twenty grand, after flights are paid for, is probably not going to last the eight months on the surfing tour, and I still haven't paid the $1500 to the ASP and registered as a competitor. I decide to go to Melbourne, to see a friend who's the marketing manager of a comedy club. I've worked for him before selling cheap tickets to live comedy shows and know I can make fast cash.

On the night before departure, I have a barbecue. Old friends arrive to see me off and everyone is in good spirits. Pizza Shop is on crutches. He confides in me that it's time for a change; he'll stop drinking and things will be different. I wish him all the best and leave the next day.

Melbourne, April

Melbourne, Australia's second-largest city, is a place with attitude. If you're to conjure up all of Melbourne's juice and put it into someone, you'll probably create a girl with pink beads in her hair, studying law by day and karate by night. Oddly, I'm entering Melbourne during the Comedy Festival—an event that immediately sparks a plethora of awkward memories.

After the flight, I take a taxi to a hostel, dump my bags and head for the Comic's Lounge. The Lounge is located in an inner-city bohemian area—the kind of place where everyone wants to be an actor or musician. The Comic's Lounge runs seven nights a week and is the biggest comedy club in Melbourne. Upstairs, there are velvet armchairs and chandeliers, an office, a bar and a 500-seat main room. Jason Carstens, my old boss, is in the office making phone calls. He's smoking and ranting in a way that's familiar, even though I haven't seen him for two years. He glances up and motions me onto a chair, as if I'm the person he's expecting to walk through the door. There are no surprised facial expressions, no bear hugs, no dramatics. Instead, he continues with the call: 'Bloody hell mate, why on earth did you book him? I'd get more laughs at a funeral.'

He ends the phone call and leans back in his chair.

'Mate,' he says, 'you're back.'

'Hi Jas, how are ya?'

'Not bad. You?'

'Pretty good. Any chance of a bit of work?'

'Ha,' he cries, and claps his hands together. 'God love you Sully.'

'No, seriously . . .'

'Seriously what? You come in here after two years in the wilderness and demand a job.'

He looks me up and down with a grin. 'When do you want to start?'

'As soon as possible.'

'Okay, I'll see you here on Monday morning.'

'Thanks,' I say, and turn to leave.

'Sully,' he says, as I'm halfway out the door. 'What are ya doin' tonight?'

'Not much, probably just going to bed early.'

'Come down to the Exford. I'm hosting a late-night show for the Comedy Festival.'

'Okay, but I'm not performing.'

'I didn't ask you to. The show starts at ten.'

I go back to the hostel, have a shower and think about

possibilities, wondering if things will be like the good old days. The showers in the hostel are communal and, on the way back to my room, I see a girl sitting down and reading. Even though I'm out of form with idle chat, I have an urge to talk to her. She doesn't seem to notice me standing there, or maybe she does and pretends not to—either way she continues reading.

'How's the book?'

It's the most obvious opener and she knows it.

'It's okay.'

'Where are you from?'

'Sweden.'

'I was in Norway two years ago.' Surprise surprise, I had to say it.

'What part?'

'Stavanger.'

She looks up at me.

'What were you doing in Stavanger?'

'I was teaching surfing.' (Actually I went to Norway to chase down a girl and gave two surfing lessons to curious students but now is not the time for the truth.)

'I didn't know there is surf in Norway,' she says, puzzled.

'There is,' I state, and my brain races for the names of the beaches in case she asks.

She doesn't. A pause lingers. It is time to take a risk.

'The Comedy Festival's on in Melbourne at the moment.'

'Really?'

This is my best hand—Scandinavians are usually university educated and interested in the arts.

'I'm going to a show tonight, you can come along if you want.'

'Thanks, but I don't have much money at the moment.'

'No problem, it's free.'

She glances up and smiles. I have her cornered.

'Okay,' she says, and we arrange to meet in 30 minutes.

The girl's name is Leena. I catch a tram with her to the gig and ask the kind of light questions all travellers get: Where have you been so far and where are you going next? We dismount the tram at Russell Street and walk the few blocks to the Exford.

Inside there are about 20 people at the bar. One of these, Jason, is negotiating free drink cards with the manager. I say hello to him then watch as he attempts to capture the crowd's attention to start the show. I glance around the room—nothing has changed. The comedy is free to anyone who stumbles upon it, so various people (inner-city bankers, students, drug dealers) often drop by in various states of inebriation. The comedy is performed in the corner of the room; there's no stage or spotlight. There is a microphone, but the sound from it is barely enough to drown out bar talk. It is, I believe, the hardest venue in which to perform stand-up comedy in Australia.

The show runs like a variety night, with comedians giving ten-minute samples of their Festival gig. They talk about all the usual comedian fodder: Saddam Hussein, the problems with America, the problems with Australia, the problems with their relationships.

Jason is the compere and starts off with a routine about the deaf Olympics that I've heard so many times I could jump up and perform it for him. In the break he buys me a beer and I tell him about my plan to go on the surfing tour. He asks about the crowd response to his jokes and I give positive feedback. And then, of course, the conversation veers toward the thing that I'm most afraid of.

'So man, you doin' a gig or what?'

'Nah, not tonight.'

'But I need ya, I've had two comedians pull out.'

'Sorry Jas, I can't.'

'Give me one good reason?'

'I'll give you three. One, because I've got nothing prepared. Two, because I'm trying to impress a Swedish girl, and three, because the last time I performed here I promised myself I never would again.'

'Look,' he says with disgust, 'just shut up and do a gig.'

'Jas, I seriously believe I'm not funny,' I confess. (It is the truth.)

'Well I'm going to be introducing ya, so you better come up with somethin'.'

He walks off. I know him well enough to know the threat is real. My mind scatters for funny ideas. I try to remember little jokes and impressions that I've used before. Slumped against the bar, watching rowdy men, I wonder why I ever wanted to be a comedian.

I started two weeks before my 21st birthday. It seemed like the right time. Like most 20-year-olds, my thoughts were skewed to the left and I had a few issues with the world. If I was the smallest puppy in the pet store, then stand-up presented itself as the best way to get attention.

My first gig at a smoky little comedy club in Sydney went disastrously. In five minutes I did not get one laugh and left the stage to wallow in a state of alarming self-despair. It took me eight months to build up the courage to do it again and when I did, I was worse. I stumbled upon laughter, accidentally, on my third attempt. At that point, I had conned the owner of a 500-seat venue on the Gold Coast for a five-minute spot. It started badly again; I felt fed up with the crowd and told them so, and they shocked the hell out of me by laughing back. After that third gig I was hooked and became a regular around comedy clubs. Over the years I performed in America, England, New Zealand and Edinburgh, and honed my act to the point where I could rely on a few laughs but it was never ground-breaking. If Lenny Bruce is the Rolling Stones of stand-up, then I'm the pub band playing covers in the corner.

Jason introduces me as 'a good mate who's performed all around the world'.

I give everything in the first few minutes (including overused impressions of George Bush), then quickly run out of steam. Drawing a blank, I make a joke about John Howard. The crowd, while not necessarily fans of the prime minister, are drunk and not prepared to listen to a political rant dressed up as comedy. They heckle and I try my best at comebacks but leave with a sense of defeat, overpowered by shouting from the bar.

'Almost had 'em,' says Jason in the break, passing me a beer.

'Yeah, probably shouldn't have gone political.'

'Probably not.'

'Have you seen Leena?' I ask.

We look around but there's no sight of her.

'She probably left after hearing your jokes,' he says, and then thinks it's funny enough to mention to the crowd while introducing the next performer.

'Hey, the last comedian's girlfriend just left him 'cos you guys didn't laugh, so let's show some love for ...'

After the show, the comedians cash in their drink cards. We're all full of the same insecurities and self-deprecating jokes fly around the group. By his fifth bourbon and coke, Jason is in a lethal mood. He has a hat full of hilarious rants about the problems with the Melbourne comedy scene. As he often mentions, he was raised as a 'barefoot kid in the council flats of Prahran' and he saves his best taunts for the new crop of university-educated comedians.

'Yeah, I know they look cool as they prance around in front of the spotlight,' he says, 'but can they do me a favour, can they tell me a fucking joke?'

We walk to a bar in the city centre which is the social hub of the Comedy Festival. Inside there are swarms of comedians. We spot the manager of the Comic's Lounge, Grant Lee, and join him at the bar.

Grant is young, big and boisterous. He has been given the job of running the Comic's Lounge after his dad left. Jason and Grant work together at the Lounge during the day; Jason runs the marketing department and Grant books the acts. If there is a word more extreme than dysfunctional, it would describe the relationship between them. The round of drinks we order is a mistake. The pressure on them to run the Comic's Lounge has caused stress and the combination of alcohol spurs a massive argument. I offer advice and end up in the middle of it. At one point, Grant has me pinned against the wall with his hands around my neck.

'Do you think I give a fuck what you think?' he yells. 'You come in and out of the Lounge every few years and walk around like your shit don't stink.'

I decide not to mention starting work there on Monday.

'Look mate,' Jason interrupts diplomatically, 'we're trying to run a comedy club and he's going on a surfing tour. We've just got different agendas, that's all.'

As quickly as the argument starts, it stops, and the three of us go to the Crown Casino, which is another mistake because I know both of them are mad gamblers. In less than an hour Jason has lost $400 and is bashing a poker machine. Six security men attempt to drag him out but he doesn't go easily, yelling the entire way to the door. Outside, they throw him to the ground.

'Don't manhandle me, don't manhandle me,' he shouts. 'Everything's on camera.'

By now, a large crowd has gathered.

'Hey mate, who is that?'a passer-by asks me, pointing at Jason.

'My boss.'

I've moved onto Jason's couch. Jason lives in a little flat across the road from the Comic's Lounge. Inside, there is a small kitchen stocked with vegetarian food, a bedroom where he sleeps, a tiny office which stores sales figures, and a lounge room, which is used for motivational meetings by day and is a place for myself and a dog called Floyd to sleep at night.

In the afternoon we go to a football game. At the ground we meet Grant, who greets us both with enthusiasm. There's no mention of the night before.

Australian Rules football is a bizarre game. Basically, 18 men run around beating the crap out of each other in the guise of following a football. Unlike other sports, heckling the players is not only permitted but encouraged. Jason and Grant watch the game in a state of insanity, shouting at the players and peppering the umpires with abuse. They save their worst for the coach of the team they support.

'Bloody hell Wallace, just 'cos ya got a clipboard and pen doesn't mean anyone should listen to ya.'

I sit back and laugh and wonder why I'm always attracted to these types—the types that like to wail in a country that likes to wait.

After the game I go to Richmond to meet Harry Keiffe. Harry's a funny bloke; he gave up a law degree to concentrate on stand-up comedy, and now works during the day as a travel agent. His real name is Aaron Kieffe but he calls himself Harry because of an uncanny likeness to Harry Potter. Last time I was in Melbourne I remember reading a review about his show titled 'Life as a 30-year-old professional who looks like a 15-year-old wizard' and was surprised that he'd managed to build a whole act around this, and even more surprised that the review was positive.

Inside the travel agency, Harry is in professional mode. He wears a white shirt and tie, sports an eager grin, and has glasses and dark hair (actually, he really does look like Harry Potter). He greets me happily and we catch up. I tell him about my plans for the surfing tour and he checks prices on around-the-world tickets, vowing to find the best deal. The first competition I'm planning to enter in Durban (Mr Price Pro) is not for another five weeks, so I decide to buy a ticket to Indonesia. My training schedule in Australia has failed dramatically and, having surfed in Indonesia before, I know the waves are good this time of the year—and a diet of rice and fish will do no harm to a bulging waist.

Later, I catch a tram to the Exford where Jason cons

me into performing again. This time a respectable-looking lady heckles me. She wears a pinstriped suit and is sitting with a group of women who look like they're on the final stretch of a girls' night out.

'Well, if you can do better, why don't you have a go?' I say, and offer her the microphone. To my surprise she takes it.

She stands up and tells a joke about having sex with a chicken. For the punchline, she actually spits feathers from her mouth. I look on astonished, wondering how a lady who's probably an accountant during the day can premeditate such a joke. For starters, where did she get the feathers? But it's just another night at the Exford. The crowd laughs. We all get drunk. We all go home.

The following day I start work. After piling my clothes under the couch, a meeting begins in the lounge room. Jason gives a typically fiery speech about the importance of goals and discipline, then introduces me to the other reps and tells flattering stories about my selling skills.

'He gave himself six months to save up enough money to get to America, after working for me he was there in four.'

I smile awkwardly and remember back to the pre-America phase, knowing things were different back then — you can achieve anything with the right mix of exuberance and innocence.

I'm given a map of an inner-city suburb, Hawthorn, to canvass. I arrive feeling hungover and tired and sit on a park bench for a few minutes, sipping an energy drink and reminding myself why I'm doing this. For motivation, I jot down all the surfing breaks I plan on going to.

The comedy tickets are sold in a sheet of six. The idea is to go directly into businesses and convince them to get a group together for a show at the Comic's Lounge in the next month. While office workers jostle past, I read over a typed script to familiarise myself. I approach a real estate agency. Inside, a girl with bright pink nails is typing feverishly.

'Hello,' I say.

She looks up, revealing a pretty face.

'How can I help?' she asks. Then she quickly adds, 'You're not selling anything are you?'

'What me, a salesman?' I mock, as if it's the most absurd thing I've ever heard.

'Look, I'm really busy,' she says, and continues typing to reiterate the point.

After a lame attempt at a pitch I'm cut off and asked to leave. I catch a tram back to the Comic's Lounge.

'What the fuck?' announces Jason at the sight of me.

'Sorry mate, I can't do it anymore.'

'What do you mean you can't do it anymore? It's selling, ya never forget it.'

'Nah, I really can't, don't ask why. I just can't.'

I know it's useless to explain the reason—things have changed, I have changed. I've given up breakdancing and Jim Carey impersonations. I've lost the urge to spark reactions from strangers. I no longer bound up the stairs of the Lounge on a Friday night, drunk on excitement, sweltering from the hustle of the day's sales and hassling management for any stage time they can give me.

'Sully,' Jason says, stubbing a cigarette in the ashtray. 'Ya come in here demanding a job. I give ya one and ya give up in ten minutes. What am I gonna tell the others? I've already said you're a gun.'

'I dunno. Look Jas, I'm sorry.'

He stays annoyed at me for a few hours but after I shamble through another ten minutes of stand-up at the Exford that night, all seems to be forgotten.

During the week I buy my round-the-world ticket. It's all set. The plan is to spend a month in Indonesia to practise surfing, and then I'll compete in South Africa, England, France, Portugal, Spain, the Canary Islands, Brazil and Hawaii.

My final night at the Exford is more manic than usual. The comedy is actually stopped mid-show after someone attempts to throw a chair on stage at Jason. This does not really surprise me. From past experience I know that sometimes people take offence to his more politically incorrect yarns. Harry arrives two hours later—at this point we're all fairly drunk but he's worse.

'What happened to the comedy?' he yells.

'We decided to cut it short for the night,' Jason informs him.

'That's bullshit. I can take this crowd,' he declares.

After switching on the microphone, he stands on a chair in the corner and bellows: 'Do any of you have any idea what it's like to be a 30-year-old ex-lawyer trapped inside the body of a 15-year-old wizard?'

'Who is that?' says a girl at the bar, nudging me with a perplexed grin.

'My travel agent.'

Indonesia, May

Indonesia is like an untamed horse. It's feverish, unpredictable, excitable, happy, crazy. If you can handle it, you'll get the ride of your life. It is my fifth time inside Bali and, like a nurse who has spent time in emergency, my senses have numbed to the madness.

I know the score at the airport: US$25 to customs, smile politely but refuse help from baggage handlers, and only change enough money for a taxi. I catch a ride with a driver called Maddi. While gazing out the window it's obvious to me that things have changed since the terrorist attacks.

'Why so quiet?' I ask Maddi.

'I don't know, perhaps Australian government. They have travel warnings.'

Maddi seems politically astute and I feel like questioning him further but there's sadness inside him. His weary eyes seem to have seen a hundred economic hardships and it doesn't feel right to waste his energy. The truth is he just wants to drop me off and scout for more business.

When I arrive at Tunjung Inn, someone rushes to the cab shouting: 'Hey Sully Sully.'

I haven't stayed at the hotel for two years but the greeting does not surprise me. Unlike Westerners, Indonesians remember names. It's a simple equation: Knowing names means tips and tips feed families. I thank Maddi for the ride, leave a tip and haul my bags to a room.

Feeling the urge to do the one thing I came for, I take off in search of surfboards. There's a little shop not far from the hotel where I've bought boards before. Inside, the owner, Yoman, recognises me and we instantly begin the Indonesian-style cat-and-mouse bartering, with ridiculous offers and counter bids. Yoman receives every offer with a brief look of shock but it's all part of the game and he jumps around the shop happily. I pull a thin 6' 4" off the rack; the kind of surfboard I rode as an 18-year-old.

'How much?'

'You want this board?'

'Yeah.'

'I don't think this board is good for you.'

'Why not?'

Yoman looks at me delicately, then says 'You too big Sully' and bursts out laughing.

I have to give it to him—he's a gutsy little bugger. Also, he has a point; I'd gone home to train and have actually left Australia 5 kilos heavier.

'Don't worry, I'm going to lose weight,' I say sheepishly.

'Okay, no problem. I sell to you for $400.'

After haggling, I get him down to $700 for two surfboards and a board bag and leave the shop in good spirits. My two boards are new but made by unknown shapers. There is a yellow round-tail, 6'6" long, and a boxy little square-tail 6'4". Back at my hotel room, I check over the boards. It seems funny to think that over the next eight months I'll be pinning my hopes on these two sticker-less boards to perform against the magnitude of the pro's sponsored custom-shaped quivers.

In the afternoon, I finally pay the $1500 WQS registration fee via credit card online, print out a copy of the registration and the Mr Price Pro entry form, and then search for a post office to send them from. On a side street, I find one where parcels fly chaotically and all money calculations are done by a clerk scribbling on a piece of paper, but he assures me the documents will arrive.

Afterwards, I hire a motorbike and ride along the beach with the new yellow round-tailed board tucked under my arm. I arrive at a little shelter. For $5, the locals will take you to a surf spot about 800 metres out called Kuta Reef. They whisk me out on a beautiful old handmade canoe and drop me 100 metres from the break.

In the surf, there are only two Americans and an old Australian. I say hello and wait my turn for a wave. The waves have good shape and a decent size. For the first 20 minutes I sit patiently to the side of the break and watch the others. Eventually, I catch a smaller one and race along it but dig a rail while turning. Although I'm surfing badly, the new board feels fast under my feet and I surf for two hours as the others catch their lifts back to shore.

Then the sun sets and the warm water bubbles around my shorts and I ponder the beauty of Indonesia and the beauty of the world. I look around and feel like the only thing in the ocean. And then I realise it's pitch black and I actually am the only thing in the ocean. Giving up on my lift, I turn around and start paddling for the bright lights of Bali. On shore, I seek out my boat driver.

'Oh sorry sir,' he says. 'I thought you were on different boat.'

I ride back to the hotel with an urge to drink, meet a Dutch pilot on leave and we pub-crawl through the bars of Kuta.

After waking with a hangover and the previous night's events running through my head like a dream, I pack my bags, check out of the Tunjung Inn, hire a motorbike and make for a beach I've stayed at before called Dreamland. Driving with one arm on the motorbike and the other clutching my two surfboards, I weave past all the usual madness. I imagine my little brother Connor with me, clinging on for dear life and treating the ride like a video game; 10 points to avoid trucks, 20 points to avoid stray dogs, 100 points to avoid the police.

About Indonesian police: It has taken me three trips to work them out. During my first time in Bali, they fined me $30 for not wearing a helmet, even though every local on a motorbike was doing the same. After my angry protests, they doubled the fine. The second time they fined me I reluctantly handed over the money. On the third time, I greeted them with an open smile, said hello in Indonesian and slapped $5 into their palms before they'd said a word. They responded with broad smiles and let me drive on. Sometimes, it just takes a while to figure out a new culture.

Dreamland is 40 minutes from Kuta and has huts stacked along the beach. It's packaged as a little patch of paradise so during the day the locals line the beach with reclining chairs and sell fruit and ice-creams to the tourists. I park the motorbike, lug my gear across the beach and say hello to Yoni, the father of the family I've previously stayed with, who owns a hut on the beach.

In the afternoon I surf a fat wave just offshore and try my best to dart numerous Malibu riders.

At night the family cooks fresh fish and rice and I swallow it down with a few bintangs and feel pretty good about the world, discussing politics with a politically minded couple from Finland who share the hut. After the meal we go to bed with the soft sound of waves crashing against the shore, but I can't sleep. I'm throttled by feelings of insecurity and, after stumbling out of the hut in darkness, I find a recliner left out on the beach, stare up at the stars, and have doubts about how I'll perform on the WQS. In the afternoon I'd stubbed my toe and wiped-out just trying to get to my feet on a wave. Can I really mix it with the pros? I dip my feet into the sand and fall asleep on the recliner with fresh fantasies of surfing well.

The next morning I find paradise, accidentally. While surfing Uluwatu, a famous left-hander 2 kilometres from Dreamland, I catch a long wave and turn around to see the pack of surfers so far away they appear to be small dots on the horizon. Feeling tired, I decide not to go back against the rip and instead drift with a lazy one-arm paddle until I reach the next beach, which has a sheer cliff that looks too steep to scale. I scamper up the beach and drop on the sand feeling exhausted. I see a little track. It's actually a concrete pathway that someone has built which winds vertically up the cliff. I climb it and discover a hotel at the top.

'Excuse me,' I say to an old lady making a necklace. 'Do you know if I can walk back to Uluwatu?'

She smiles but speaks little English, so calls for her daughter, who arrives and cheekily tells me she will take me back on her motorbike, but only if I book a night in the hotel.

'How much are the rooms?' I ask

'Fifty thousand rupiah.' ($7 Aussie)

It's the same price as Dreamland. I catch a ride with the girl back to Uluwatu, ride back to the hut at Dreamland to collect my stuff, and then book into the hotel on the cliff.

In the hotel there's a young American couple, three young South Africans, an old American and a young Brazilian. Everyone has discovered the place by accident and is excited with the find.

'We've got our own private beach down there,' marvels John from the couple. 'I wouldn't wanna guess what you'd pay for a place like this in the States.'

At night the family cooks an amazing seafood barbecue. There is snapper, tuna, prawns, sweet potato and Indonesian lemongrass. We pile fish on our plates, heap plaudits on the chef and toast our fortune.

No doubt already feeling heady with the atmosphere, Chiago, the Brazilian, disappears into the night and returns with fireworks and magic mushrooms. (A combination of elements certain to spark a quick trip to an Indonesian hospital.) We're an hour from Kuta and essentially in the middle of nowhere but no one questions him. In Indonesia, you can buy the dandruff off a jungle monkey for a price.

A bonfire is made on the beach and the party kicks into life. Everyone eats the magic mushrooms except me. They've changed my life before and I don't feel like a second redirection. The family joins us on the beach and the young children dance. Every fizz from the fireworks through the night sky is received with a cheer. In my sober state, I notice how people react to the mushrooms; the South Africans laugh and joke, the couple start deep conversations, the old man talks to himself and Chiago dances dangerously close to the fire. I stay and watch the loonies for an hour, then go to bed as the voices from the beach reverberate around the cliffs.

In the morning I crash my hired motorbike. Riding back from Uluwatu, I round a gravel bend and spot someone coming the other way. In an attempt to dodge him I go flying off the road.

'Shit, you alright mate?' the guy asks with concern.

It's another Australian.

'Yeah,' I reply shakily.

But there's a cut on my leg and scratches up my arm, a hole in my board, and the motorbike's handlebars are twisted. I ride gingerly back to the hotel and the old lady produces a jar of red cream and applies it to my wounds.

The ride back to Kuta feels more dangerous than usual. Because of my injuries, I nurse the bike at 20 kilometres an hour, trying to keep the handlebars straight with one arm, while holding my surfboards with the other. The trip is usually an hour but I take three; the whole time with visions of a truck swiping me from the side of the road.

Eventually I make it to Kuta, buy some Chinese medicine for the cuts, drop the board at a ding-repairer, barter with the motorbike owner (giving him $50 for the damage), and search for a beer.

Re: Membership form
From: Brodie
Sent: Monday, 5 June 2006 8:53:57AM
To: Sullivan McLeod

Hi Sullivan,

I received your membership form in the mail today from Bali. Thank you for sending it again. I will process your membership payment this week and your entry.

Please check your entry has been recorded online at aspworldtour.com.

Select the tour schedule and the Mr. Price Pro and the seed list should come up. If your name is not on the list please let me know ASAP. This is a requirement of all WQS competitors.

Have fun in Bali. If you have any other questions please don't hesitate to let me know.

Kind regards,

BJC
ASP Australasia Administration
Surfing Australia

Grajagan, June

Kuta is to Australians what Teneriffe is to Brits. There are bars open all night, beaches where you can pick up anything from a pineapple juice to a crossbow, and a heck of a lot of debauchery. I spend three days healing my wounds there but feel the urge to leave — there's only so long that you can look down upon drunk shirtless Australians before you feel like joining them, and I'm desperate to be fit for the WQS.

So I book a ticket to G-land. G-land is short for Grajagan, which is an island off Java with one of the most famous waves in the world. Like every surfer, I grew up with pictures of the wave filtering through my home in surfing magazines and always wanted to go. Initially, there was only one surf camp that catered for rich surfers, but these days the average surfer can afford it, so I book the cheapest package. For $400 I get the trip there, accommodation for a week and three meals a day.

'The bus will leave here at midnight in four days,' the kid behind the counter informs me.

'No worries.'

'Sir,' he says, looking at me sternly, 'you know big waves are coming?'

'Big, what do you mean big?'

'Very big waves. You must buy big board.'

With apprehension, I check the internet and discover the kid is right. They are predicting the biggest swell that has hit Indonesia in a year. Feeling under-equipped, I go back to Yoman's surf shop and buy a third board—this one big enough to deal with the conditions. It's 7' 10", wide and yellow, and I feel proud with it under my arm as I walk past sunburnt tourists shopping for CDs and sarongs.

'Oi,' someone yells, and I turn around and see Morgs, a friend of my cousin. His back is leaning against the wall of a restaurant and a BB-gun is clutched to his chest. Remarkably, not only was he in exactly the same place when I saw him two years ago here in Bali but he was doing exactly the same thing—hiding from friends who were shooting BB-guns. (This ia a type of toy gun only legal in Indonesia that can cause serious pain from close range.)

The boys are happy to see me (they have a new target) and encourage me to move into their hotel.

'You should see the chicks at this place,' Morgs says.

And so it begins—four days of alcohol poisoning camouflaged by poolside dancing with Scandinavian girls to Beatles tunes. In the midst of the blur, while I'm drunk in boxer shorts, Morgs approaches me in the pool.

'Hey mate, weren't you going to G-land at 12 o'clock tonight?'

'G-land, shmeeland. I'm stayin' 'ere,' I say, my beer-drenched words delivered less clearly than intended.

'Mate, if I was you I'd go. That trip was 400 bucks and your bus leaves in ten minutes.'

Cursing, I jump out of the pool, pack my things, and rush out of the hotel soaking wet.

I just make the bus, slump beside someone and look around. The men on board share an expression of determination, as if expecting a rough trip. If anyone knew how rough at this point, I'm sure a few of us would jump out and join the throng of wild prostitutes parading along the streets of Kuta.

Our driver's sombrero hat barely reaches the dashboard. His driving is high on courage and low on logic.

'Fark,' says Chris, an American sitting beside me, as we lurch past a truck while rounding a corner. 'This guy can't be serious.'

None of us are brave enough to chance sleep and through the night we grip our seats as if on a never-ending rollercoaster.

With the rising sun, we arrive at a port and the driver negotiates our way onto a large ship. On board it looks like a scene from a Buster Keaton film; chickens squawk, pigs squeal and barefoot men smoke cigarettes precariously close to barrels of petrol.

'Good idea to stay on bus,' the driver says; his first words since Kuta.

The first thing we do is jump off the bus. On the top deck, a little kid runs up to me.

'Mister, Mister, if I jump from the boat you throw money?'

'Orright,' I reply, not actually expecting him to.

But he suddenly takes off his shirt and launches into the ocean. Soon, other kids do the same. I look down at the scene knowing that if someone offers me $1000, I will still not jump from the boat, and kids no older than twelve are bobbing on the surface because of the half-promise of a few bucks.

We throw money at the kids, which they collect and keep in their mouths. From the deck of the boat, I motion to the kid who first approached me, the smallest, to swim away from the others and I roll up a 50 000 rupiah note and drop it into his eager hands.

When the engines kick into life, the kids casually grab the side of the boat and are dragged into the ocean. A kilometre out, while plunged against the rolling swells, they let go and swim towards another ship heading back. The oldest and strongest of the group intercepts the passing ship and grabs on, then the next eldest makes it, but the youngest struggles; his arms flail through the powerful swells.

I'm concentrating so hard I don't notice Chris, the American, who lets out a sharp breath beside me. Then, like a scene from a Spielberg movie, two kids link arms and form a chain and the smallest kid clutches the outstretched hand and is dragged back with the boat. I look back wistfully. One of the craziest things I've ever seen is just another day for the Indonesian kids.

After the boat ride the bus driver puts our lives in danger for another three hours until we reach a small beach. We carry our boards across the sand and greet the driver of a speedboat, who's our lift to Grajagan.

'Big waves, hold on,' he says; the only words needed to let us know the journey isn't over.

He takes off for a little pass in the reef and guns towards an oncoming wave, which we hit and launch skywards. At one point, the only part of my body connected to the boat is my hand on a railing. In midair time slows and I look down to see others desperately hugging whatever they can. And then the boat lands and we're crunched back on deck. With the good news of nobody overboard, the captain smiles and heads towards another wave with gusto.

We arrive in Grajagan an hour later. A bearded American, who I later discover is the camp manager, comes bounding from the jungle.

'Holy shit,' he says, 'I can't believe you guys made it.'

As we wearily trudge up the sand, he tells us about the camp.

'Hey good news,' he says, grinning. 'Get yourselves settled and wax up. G-land is 10 to 12 foot and firing and we've got a boat that'll take you there in half an hour.'

Even by Indonesian standards, it has been a hell of a trip. I share a bamboo hut with Chris and drop on a bed, exhausted.

'What on earth are you doing?' says Chris, startled. 'Didn't you just hear the guy? G-land is 10 feet and pumping, let's go surfing.'

'I don't think so bro, I've had two hours sleep in the past two days.'

The truth is I feel scared. I don't want to surf massive tubes over a shallow reef on an unknown board at an unknown break.

'Jesus Christ!' Chris shouts. 'This is why we came here. Do I have to drag your sorry ass out there?'

'Orright orright, I'm coming,' I say, and wonder about the possibility of changing room-mates.

The boat whisks us out behind the break. I see thick fast swells surging through the ocean and the spray flying off the waves, but it's hard to determine the size. We arrange a time to be picked up, jump off the boat and paddle towards the waves.

The surf is huge. I watch Chris turn and stroke into a massive chunk of water. He springs to his feet and slides down the face, but it's too steep and his board nose-dives into the wave. After the wave crashes upon him, I see his board tombstoning in a froth of water.

I'm relieved when he breaks the surface, shakes his head and paddles back. I catch a few of the smaller ones, which are still big, and race along the face of the waves before flicking out. The new 7' 10" board is bigger than I'm used to but the extra foam makes paddling easier and it feels steady under my feet. With the adrenalin pumping, the chaotic trip feels like a distant memory.

As the sun sets, I paddle for a small one, miss it, and turn to see massive waves on the horizon. As the pack scratches frantically for the channel, I realise I'm in that horrible position, not knowing whether to paddle out to make it under them, or turn around and paddle in. When the surfers drift over the first wave, I see Chris glance over his shoulder at my impending doom.

The first wave is a creature of beauty. I watch mesmerised as it pitches and lands a few feet from me. Then I submerge and brace. As the wave collapses above me, I hear the 'ping' of my leg rope snapping and realise the board is gone. And then, like a rag-doll in a washing machine, I'm thrashed relentlessly. I come up short of breath and cop another one on the head. This time the whitewater slams me into the reef. Normally, getting caught inside is survivable because the waves will drag you in, but at G-land, the waves actually gain in size and momentum as they push along the reef.

With the last of the light I see my boat pick up the others and disappear towards shore. As darkness closes in and the pounding continues, I feel my energy drop. It's funny, the thoughts that go through your head before dying. I feel less afraid and more hopeless. Less fearful and more ridiculous. I imagine the headlines in the papers back home — surfer loses life off remote Indonesian island.

With a final effort I swim down the face of a wave in the darkness and bodysurf it as far as possible. I allow myself to be washed over the reef and half-swim half-walk across it, feeling every cut as my feet hit the coral. Drained of every ounce of energy, I eventually make it to shore, lie on the sand, peer up at the stars and thank God I'm alive.

Back in the hut, Chris greets me with relief. 'Bro, we were about to send out the search party.'

'Yeah I know, I got hammered,' I say and slump on a bed.

'Hey good news, someone found your board.'

'Really?'

'Yeah, they saw it floating in the channel and have left it at the camp.'

'I might go and pick it up.'

'Hey man,' he says, and grabs my shoulders as I'm half-way out the door. 'I told that boat driver to wait, I really did.'

I thank him, retrieve my board, and have my best sleep in years.

At G-land the waves are good for the rest of the week but never as big as the first day. Between surfs, we hang around the surprisingly well-organised camp; there is a boat which ferries us daily to the surf, pool tables, surf movies, a chess board, breakfast with fresh pineapples and bananas, and cold beers. We fall into a routine; surf after breakfast, have lunch, play a game of pool, play chess, surf in the afternoon, have dinner, sleep.

I discover more about Chris: He's smart and quick-witted, lives on the island of Maui in Hawaii, has just finished a degree in meteorology and dreams of being a television weatherman. Like most male surfers, we quickly discover our strengths and weaknesses and our friendship flourishes with competitive quests—he's better at chess and I'm better at pool. If there is a chink in Chris's armour, it's that he's quick-tempered and sometimes snaps when losing and I take pleasure in goading him. When playing chess in the afternoons, for example, he usually establishes a winning position, but knowing our ride to go surfing is leaving, I stretch the game, often taking five minutes per move. Usually Chris will watch my lethargy with frustration and when the boat driver tells us he's leaving, he'll snap: 'Hurry up jackass.'

In a week of chess we never make it past stalemate.

The other thing I like to do with Chris is make pointless lists. For example: 'Hey Chris, who are the ten best rock and roll singers of all time?' or 'Hey Chris, what are the ten best books written in the twentieth century?'

Oddly, instead of ignoring me, he always answers the questions thoughtfully and I always argue with his choices.

On the bus trip back to Kuta I spend hours pushing him to his limits.

'Are you telling me,' I say with disbelief, 'that "That's not a knife, now that's a knife" from *Crocodile Dundee* does not make your top ten quotes?'

Eventually, when I put the cricketer Don Bradman ahead of Muhammad Ali in 'the top ten sportsmen', he snaps and moves to a different seat.

'Mate,' another surfer says to me when we stop for petrol, 'can you stop winding Chris up?'

'Okay,' I reply, and for the rest of the trip we listen to music and drink beer.

At the hotel with the party pool in Kuta, nothing has changed. Morgs and the boys are still inebriated and happily shooting themselves with BB-guns. At the sight of a shimmering pool and good-looking girls, Chris forgives me and we make plans for the night.

The night is a blur. I sing karaoke at a bar, dance with a local girl at a nightclub, swim naked at the hotel and wake covered in BB-gun welts.

The next morning I catch a ferry with the mother of all hangovers to an island off Bali called Nusa Lembongan. I stay there for a week surfing two beautiful right-handers. In the hotel, the other tourists are two amicable middle-aged Australians and a Dutch couple.

One night we discover there's a television in another hotel, so we go and watch Australia play Japan in the World Cup. As a small gecko rushes across the screen, we shout support at the players and drink bintangs. It's a dramatic game which Australia wins 3–1, and afterwards, we sing songs and dance with the locals.

At the end of the week I catch a ferry back to Kuta, spend a night catching up with Chris, and then leave for the airport. The Mr Price Pro in Durban is due to start in two weeks. It's time to get serious about the WQS. Still, I feel relaxed and satisfied with my time spent surfing in Indonesia, considering it useful training. At the airport, I even feel relatively confident with my body. I'm happy with my shiny brown arms and even happier when I step on a set of scales in the airport foyer and discover I'm 5 kilos lighter.

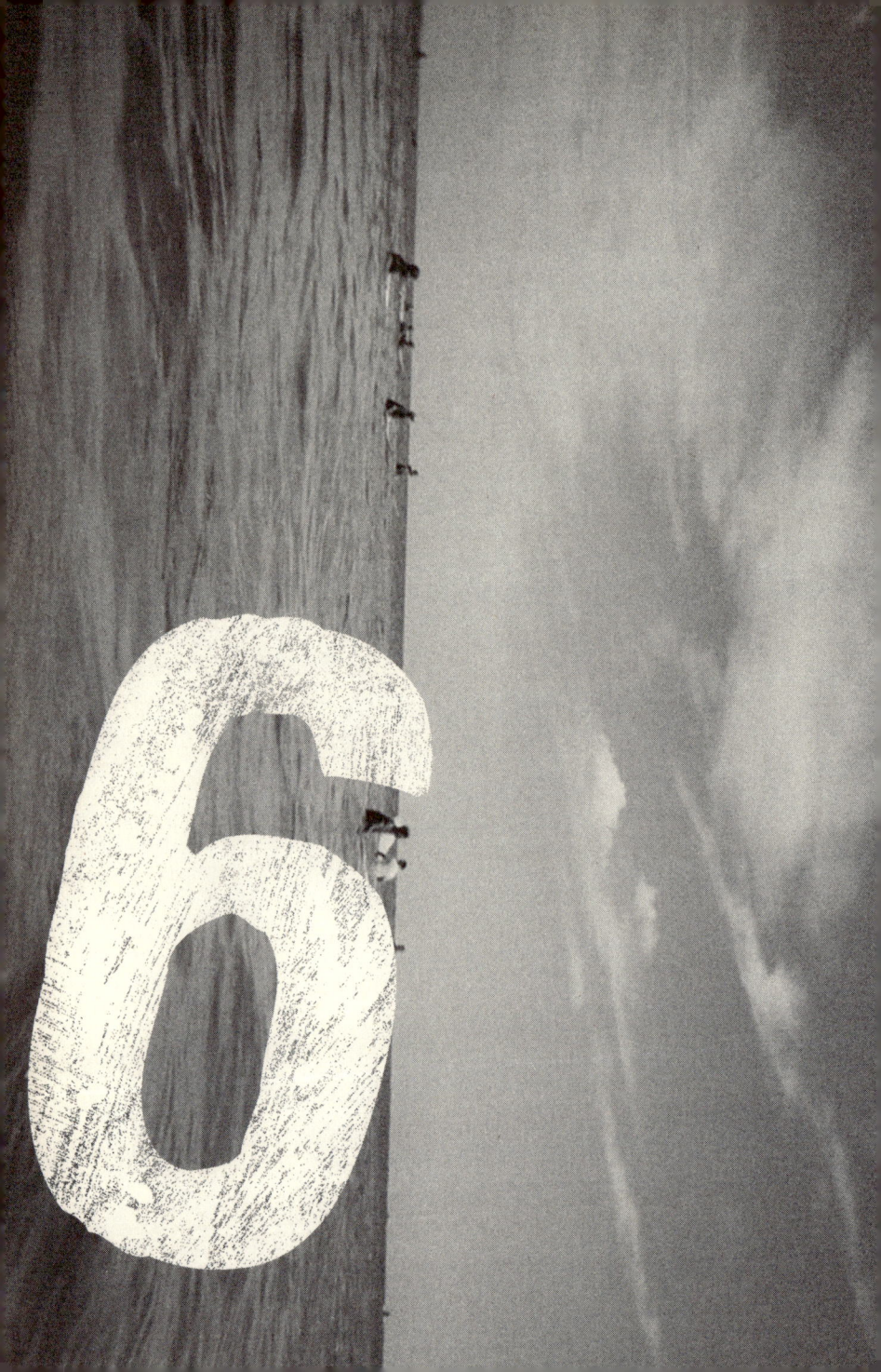

South Africa, Mid June–September

The plane trip to South Africa is long and uneventful, and gives me enough time to read a few surfing magazines. We stop briefly in Johannesburg, I never leave the airport, and then we fly to Durban.

At the airport in Durban, I chat to a sweet old lady who recommends that I stay in a hostel called Banana Backpackers. When we arrive at the hostel, the shuttle bus driver drops me off quickly and seems keen to leave. Across the road are two seedy-looking escort agencies. Inside the hostel, steel bars block the reception. From now on I decide to question advice given from sweet old ladies at airports. But the rooms are cheap ($15 Aussie a night for your own room) and the girl checking me in is friendly. Exhausted from the journey, I fall asleep to the rattle of some kind of street hustling outside.

In the morning I wake to the sound of gunshots.

'Did you hear the gunshots this morning?' I ask the

girl at reception, careful to deliver the question casually between mouthfuls of cornflakes.

'Gunshots. What gunshots?'

'The gunshots this morning.'

'Oh no,' she explains with a smile. 'That was just a car backfiring.'

I study the girl's face. She appears serious. I've spent a whole adolescence around dodgy Holdens and have never heard one go off like that.

The ten-minute trek to the beach I name 'running the gauntlet'. There are half-built concrete buildings which house squatters, people lurking around escort agencies and others selling watches and sunglasses from roadside stalls.

Once at the beach, however, the atmosphere changes. There are surf shops, restaurants, bars and a boardwalk where white people stroll around like extras from an American soap show.

The waves are small and crumbly and break between a series of jetties. In the sunshine I dangle my legs from a jetty and watch the surfers, feeling confident that my ability will compare. After all, Australians beat South Africans at rugby and cricket—how good could they be at surfing? However, after watching a kid no older than 14 make four re-entries and an air 360, I re-evaluate. I watch the surfers with amazement. Most surf with speed, power and flair and are as good, if not better, than the best from Margaret River. Little did I know then, that on a small beach break between two jetties, I've stumbled upon the cream of South African surfing warming up for the contest.

On the way back to the hostel I'm robbed by a guy called Maurice. He approaches me with idle banter, asking why I've come to South Africa. I tell him I'm here for the surfing competition and he spends ten minutes describing life in South Africa, then says: 'Look bro, I hate to do this, but another thing I do here is rob people.'

'Really?' I reply, feeling a lump form in my throat. 'Am I being robbed?'

'Actually you are. Don't look now but there's a guy 5 metres behind us with a knife. You seem like a cool cat, just hand over whatever you can.'

'Is 50 rand enough?' ($10 Aussie)

'Yeah, that's cool man,' he replies and offers a high five (which I return!?). 'Hey, good luck in the Mr Price, I'll be cheering for ya.'

With reflection, the robbing is a bummer but fits conveniently with my new mantra, 'every cloud has a silver lining'. When things go wrong I like to chant 'Every cloud, every cloud.'

The next day I half-walk half-run through the gauntlet clutching my yellow round-tail surfboard, careful not to make eye contact with anyone. At the beach the swell has picked up. Powerful rights run for hundreds of metres past the jetty and the surfers pick them off like ants on breadcrumbs. I've seen numerous documentaries on shark attacks in South Africa and mention this to another surfer before jumping in.

'You don't need to worry,' he assures me, 'this whole area is netted.'

Feeling more confident, I jump from the jetty, narrowly avoid being crushed into a concrete pylon, which would have been embarrassing because a large crowd is watching, and paddle for the line-up. In the water the surfers sit with intense expressions. Not many talk. Even less smile. I don't know what to expect from South African surfers but now it's pretty clear they're not going to extend any favours to feckless Australians.

After an hour of trying unsuccessfully to catch the scraps off the pack, I float down the line to try unsuccessfully to catch the scraps off the kids, getting dropped in on twice by a 12-year-old girl. With my pride only slightly intact, I catch one in feeling tired. Somehow, I've managed to lose three weeks of Indonesian conditioning in three days.

Onshore, there's the kind of entrenched surf scene that makes the Gold Coast of Australia seem humble in comparison. A good way of judging a surf scene is counting the number of ways people choose to wear their hats. Outside the surf shop at New Pier, I count five (hat forward, hat backward, hat to the side, hat diagonally backward, hat diagonally forward).

Wanting to buy a wetsuit for the cold water in South Africa, I enter the local surf shop and meet Froggy, the quirky owner. With an expression that could either be suspicion or gentle curiosity, he asks why I'm here and, too embarrassed to let him know I've arrived for the competition, I tell him I'm just travelling around. It must have been the right answer because he quickly warms up and cracks a few of those jokes South Africans like to tell about beating Australians at rugby.

The next day Maurice, my friendly robber, visits me at the hostel with the hope of robbing me again.

'Come on man, this really isn't fair,' I say, handing over another 50 rand.

Oddly, he agrees and we come to a working arrangement: From now on he's only allowed to rob me in the 500-metre stretch between the hostel and the beach.

In the surf, it's clear the surfers from other countries have arrived for the competition. If the atmosphere was tense the day before, today it cranks further up the alpha-male meter. While paddling out, a large stingray surfaces a few feet away and scares the hell out of me.

'Don't know how he got through the shark net,' I joke to a passing surfer.

'Shark net, what shark net?'

'The shark net they put up on this beach.'

'There's no shark net,' he replies, deadpan. 'That's just something we tell the tourists to make them feel safe.'

The professionals from other countries are good but, with some pride, I discover the only surfers keeping up with the locals are Aussies, who I recognise from surfing magazines. There's Troy Brooks, a surfer from Victoria currently ranked about 20th on the WCT; James Wood, a young up-and-comer; and Mick Campbell, the veteran who was 3rd on the WCT seven years ago, but has spent four years off the tour.

Quickly giving up on catching waves, I sit in the channel being constantly fanned by spray flying off surfboards.

That afternoon I check in to the surf competition. They attach a red bracelet to my wrist and give me a T-shirt, some shaving gear, a men's magazine and wax. The red bracelet is only for competitors. I feel like an impostor wearing it and shove my hands deep in my pockets whenever a group of surfers walks past.

On the trip back, partly to hide from Maurice but mostly because of curiosity, I allow myself to be shepherded into a minibus. I'd spotted the buses on my first day in Durban and felt curious about them. Basically, they're hotted-up old vans with names like 'Love Mobile' or 'Night Owl', which drive frantically through the city. Inside, I'm the only white passenger. Loud drum and bass music pumps through the speakers and every few metres, the van stops and a very charismatic black guy jumps out and starts herding more people on board.

In Bali I'd asked a South African about South Africa and he'd replied: 'It will be different to anywhere you've been — there's more energy on land and more energy in the water.'

Looking from the window of the minibus I now understand what he meant. After 40 minutes of driving

I realise I'm going the wrong way and jump out, pay the fare and catch another bus back to my original starting point.

Later in the hostel I tell the girl at reception about riding on the minibus, letting her know that I was the only white person on board.

'Of course you were,' she replies. 'White people would never ride them.'

'Why not?'

'They're far too dangerous.'

I consider questioning her further, but resolve that there's still a lot that I don't know about South Africa.

On the day before the Mr Price Pro, I meet a guy called Will at the hostel and he invites me to a famous horse race called the Durban July. Of course, if I have any sort of discipline, I'll say no. If my decision-making process has any reasonable logic, I'll say no. If my name isn't Sullivan McLeod and I haven't spent 29 years going anywhere with a hint of girls and beer, I'll say no.

I go to the track and barely see a horse. The day is spent drinking and trying to schmooze beautiful South African girls in lacy frocks. Later, even though I have no memory of it, I enter the thirteenth race. (Where a herd of pissed blokes do a lap of the track naked.)

I wake in the morning at the hostel wearing a tight pink T-shirt and cowboy hat and feeling like my brain has been stolen in the night and beaten by thugs. My tongue is caked with fur.

At the beach, a large crowd has gathered to watch the surfers compete in dribbly 1-foot surf. I enter the competitors' area feeling one part foreboding guilt and three parts foolishness. When I attempt to check in, a pleasant organiser informs me of what I already suspect— that I've missed my heat.

'We delayed it for two hours,' he explains, 'but we had to run it, I'm sorry.'

A story: When I was 19, after a weekend visiting my family in Margaret River, my brother Ash and I wanted to go back to Perth for work. A small argument about the best way to travel turned into a massive fight—as brothers do — and we made a bet on who could hitchhike there the quickest. After giving him a five-minute start, I stuck my thumb out and a car stopped—a middle-aged lady who, remarkably, lived on the street behind me in Perth, was willing to take me the whole way.

During the ride the lady told stories about the afterlife, fate and destiny. She was a fortune teller and, I guess because we were getting along, she offered a free reading. Feeling sceptical of anything that I couldn't see or reason with, I politely declined. After stopping at a petrol station, however, she suddenly turned to me and said: 'You'll do a lot of travelling.'

'Really?'

At the time I had a secure job in Perth as a sales rep for

a dishwashing detergent company and had no intention of leaving.

'When will I travel?'

'In two years.'

Now this did interest me — how did she account for the two-year gap?

'Will I travel with anyone?'

'Yes, for a while, but for the most part you'll be by yourself.'

Having arrived in Perth before Ash and winning the bet, I forgot about her predictions and thanked her for the ride. Exactly two years later I bought a round-the-world ticket and spent the next five years travelling, mostly by myself but also with a friend.

And so, with the snake of destiny, the floating seed of hope and the random beat of chance, as I watch the Mr Price Pro in a residue of my own inept solitude, cursing my continually hopeless ways, I'm not surprised that the first person to sit beside me is a life coach who seems content to nurse me through my silly decisions.

His name is Eric. He's tall and lanky and, at first, starts with questions about the surfing competition. I tell him my story, that I've slept through my heat, and he tells me his, that he's writing a book based on four years travelling around Africa studying the human condition.

'Do you think I did the right thing going to the horse race?' I ask him.

'I don't know. Did you want to go to the horse race?'

'Yeah, but what's the point of coming all this way and missing the competition?'

'I'm not sure. How important is the competition to you?'

His question jolts a memory into my mind. I was 13, in the foyer of a cinema in Perth with my brother Jack and our parents.

'What movie do you want to see?' our parents asked us.

Although we had no idea what it was about, we chose a movie called *Point Break*. My parents went to see a different movie. Inside the cinema, Jack and I settled into our seats, sipping Coke contently.

The movie started with what was, and still is, incredible water footage of surfing. Years later we would laugh about how silly the movie was. It was clearly an attempt by Hollywood to capture how they thought surfers should be. The surfers spoke in clichés, the actors overacted and some of the flaws were obvious—you can't be riding goofy-foot on a small left-hand wave, for example, and then on the next frame be riding regular foot on a big right. But as a 13-year-old I overlooked the mistakes for the plot. Oh man, what a plot; a gang of surfers robbed banks in California so they could continue surfing around the world. While the surfers were being tracked by the FBI, there were car chases, there were explosions, there were bank robberies, there was reckless skydiving from aeroplanes but, most importantly, the motivation behind it all was to continue surfing.

It was dark when we left the cinema and as I walked with my brother through the city, we chatted and laughed about the movie. As a 13-year-old, I already liked anything that was anti the authority, so the idea of surfers robbing banks was certain to appeal. I remember having the urge to get back to Margaret River quickly. I'd missed the waves. At that moment all I wanted to do was surf.

While talking to Eric, I understand his conversation technique. By responding to my questions with questions, I was made to think about my actions and realise, on the large scale, they're not important. I feel a warm glow talking to him. He's only a few years older than me but has made many discoveries about people—that people like to talk rather than listen, people like to entertain rather than be entertained, and people like to love rather than be loved.

As quickly as Eric arrives, he disappears, vaguely mentioning something about going back to the city. I watch him walk off like an apparition and if I wasn't feeling better about myself, it'd be hard to know that our conversation has taken place.

The surfing competition runs for the rest of the week in small beach breaks. Unfortunately, the main sponsor of the event, Mr Price, is a discounted clothing chain with little knowledge of surf conditions. Presumably reasoning that more people will see their banners, they move the competition away from the long rights to crumbly peaks at the centre of the beach. Apart from the final day everyone, including myself, pays little attention to the surf contest—it's part of a beach festival and there are other things to be distracted by. There's a skateboard competition, dance party, live music and food stalls which line the boardwalk selling corn and ice-cream.

On the final day, I'm all alone watching the surfing contest in the competitors' area when a short stocky redhead, who looks like Mick Campbell, sits beside me. I introduce myself and discover it is Mick Campbell. I can't believe my luck. After reading stories about him in surfing magazines, I've always wanted to meet him.

Mick Campbell has an incredible story. He finished third on the WCT seven years ago but ended the tour to try out as a boxer. After a few years only getting local bouts in RSL clubs, he's returning to pro surfing. At 33, he's competing on the WQS with the goal of qualifying for the WCT in his first year. It's difficult to describe how hard this will be; not only has he been away from professional surfing for years but he's also lost all ratings points (points that are accrued on the previous year of the WQS to determine seeding), so he has to start most events in the trials. In many of the competitions, even to reach the finals he'll have to advance though about eight heats. But I quickly realise that if anyone can do it, it's him. Earlier this morning, surfing in conditions more favourable to light Brazilians than beefy Australians, he'd made it as far as the quarters before being knocked out.

Mick Campbell looks Australian and talks Australian.

When I mention going to a restaurant the night before and ordering a 400-ounce steak, he quips: 'Yeah, but I bet when they brought it out it looked 500.'

His stocky body is covered with fair skin and freckles. Strawberry blonde hair sprouts from the top of his forehead. When answering questions, his pale eyes dance equally with intensity and humour. I doubt if Mick even has a major surfing sponsor these days. Tanned blond kids now carry the major labels and he no longer fits the mould. But this does not seem to bother him—he rests his ragged shoes against a railing for anyone to see. There's something about the underdog that's incredibly likeable and as underdogs go, they don't come more likeable than Mick.

I have a thousand questions to ask him but, not wanting to come across as overzealous, I talk with him for 20 minutes and then watch the final. The final is between a South African, Ricky Basnett, who's a damn good surfer I've seen in the Margaret River contest, and an Australian, Dayyan Neve, who I've vaguely heard about from surfing magazines. Knocked out in the semis are Neco Padaratz, a Brazilian who was relegated from the WCT last year after testing positive to steroids, and Troy Brooks. During earlier rounds Brooks has been pulling off these incredible superman airs, a manoeuvre the other competitors did not even attempt, let alone make. How he doesn't reach the final I'll never know—probably it's a South African conspiracy.

The final is held on a full tide as weak waves dribble onto the sandbank. It's not a great spectacle but Basnett makes the best of it. His lean body is better suited to flying through the flat sections of the waves and he's comfortable landing airs. Later, I discover he's the first South African to win the event in 20 years. Standing among about five hundred people, I watch the presentations. Neve wears the kind of sunglasses normally only found on fighter pilots or rock stars. On the dais they project contrasting styles; Basnett looks happy and Neve looks ridiculous.

At the after-party in a beachside pub, I watch as the surfers dance with girls. To blend in I get drunk and try my best chatting up girls but I know the truth and, maybe, so do they. I'm a fake. I stay at the bar for three hours trapped in my own analytical drunken haze. If I think these pros, with their brand names and confident banter, are idiots, why am I trying to be like them?

Maybe I've stumbled upon something deep about myself. Maybe somewhere in these thoughts live the real fragments of who I really am. Or maybe I'm just drunk.

I arrive in Cape Town on a windy afternoon. My plan is to hang in the city for a few days and then make my way to Jeffreys Bay, which has one of the best waves in the world and is the venue for a contest that starts in a week. The contest at Jeffreys is a WCT event, which means only the top 45 ranked surfers in the world can compete in it, but I feel excited about just being a spectator and the prospect of seeing guys like Kelly Slater surfing.

At the airport I meet a tall happy Norwegian called Lars. We're both looking for accommodation and I coerce him into squeezing my bulky board bag into his tiny hire car, forcing him to navigate through the unfamiliar roads of Cape Town with his head out the window. Like most Norwegians, he's pleasant and doesn't complain about it. We arrive in the city at night, park the hire car near suspicious characters, and walk to the entrance of the Cape Town Central Hostel.

'Hello?' we shout up the stairs, but there's no answer.

We're about to give up when an old man peers over the fence.

'How can I help?'

'We want to stay for the night. Are there any rooms free?' I shout.

'Nah sorry fellas,' he replies with a sinister chortle. 'Try down the road at the other hostel.'

As we walk away, a girl rushes from the hostel.

'Excuse me?' she says. 'We have rooms available if you want to stay tonight.'

Feeling confused, we grab our bags and follow the girl. The girl's name is Amanda. She's looks about 25, has red hair and glasses and an English accent.

'Don't mind Barry,' she says with a smile as we check in. 'He's a regular who gives that treatment to everyone.'

We thank her, pay for a night, and fall asleep in our rooms.

The next day I walk up a beautiful mountain ridge overlooking Cape Town in the morning and play pool with

Lars at a nearby pub in the afternoon. We play doubles against two locals called Troy and Ryan, who ask questions about where we've been so far and where we're going next.

Frankly, I'm surprised by the South Africans. As an Australian, I expect a South-of-the-Equator showdown from the young guys but they're friendly and often ask questions about Australia, especially our rugby team. For South Africans, rugby is the beating heart of their nation. Providing Australia doesn't beat them in a rugby match in the next two weeks, I realise, my passage through the country should stay smooth.

'So, you checking out the game?' Troy asks me, sipping a beer.

'What game?'

'The rugby game between South Africa and Australia, it starts in an hour.'

As the pub quickly fills, I look around at the South African jumpers and realise I'm the only Aussie inside. The game is shown on a big screen in the corner of the pub. During the pre-game festivities everybody sings their national anthem with pride. When the Australian anthem is played, the room falls silent.

Australia beats South Africa 51–3. It's the worst loss by a South African team to Australia in the entire history of South African rugby. Somehow, before, during and immediately following the match, it's known to everybody that I'm Australian. Post-game, with a hundred people baying for my blood, I down my pint and make a quick exit.

Back at the hostel I meet a quirky young American called TJ and tell him about the rugby match.

'Sounds dangerous,' he says, and lets out a prolonged whistle, 'but if you're up for it, I challenge you to something worse.'

'What's that?'

'Diving with great white sharks.'

'Why on earth would I want to do that?'

'Because I'm going tomorrow with a group of fishermen. Besides, it's not that bad, you're in a cage.'

Back in the room, Lars is lying on a bunk bed listening to music.

'Good news,' I tell him, as he takes the headphones from his ears. 'I've booked us onto a shark dive tomorrow.'

We're picked up early in the morning by two fishermen brothers called Darryl and Wayne. As they drive us through the city in an old van, we nervously ask questions about the sharks.

'So,' says Darryl, detecting my accent, 'you boys had a win yesterday eh?'

'Oh, you mean the rugby? Yeah, I guess we were a bit lucky.'

'Are you trying to tell me,' he says with an incredulous wince, 'that you attribute a score that is 51 against 3, to luck?'

'Um, maybe we did play a bit better,' I mumble.

'What?'

'I said maybe we played a bit better.'

'I think so buddy,' he says with a laugh. 'But don't worry, you'll get yours.'

We arrive at a packed harbour, carry wetsuits and diving gear across the sand, then climb on board a boat. After the motor kicks into life, we head out towards the horizon.

'Where's the cage?' shouts TJ over the engine noise.

'I think it's that thing,' I reply, pointing to a steel contraption under the hull.

'You gotta be kiddin' me — I've seen sturdier bird-cages.'

He has a point. The cage appears on the flimsy side. Of course, we aren't reassured when the brothers mention they've welded it together in their backyard at home. I wonder about the brothers. Onshore, we'd paid the arranged fee ($100) for the trip, but there are no brochures or paraphernalia on board and it doesn't feel like the typical tourist tour. The only person who seems genuinely excited about the prospect of diving with sharks is Lars, who eagerly snaps photos from the side of the boat.

When the boat slows between two islands crammed with seals, the humming sound of the engine stops and we rock gently with the waves. The wind is cold, the water is murky, the sky is grey and the only noise to be heard is the splash of seals as they jump from rocks.

'They call this place Death Valley,' states Wayne, sniffing the air with what seems to be carnal satisfaction.

Darryl scoops a bucket into a barrel of blood and tuna oil and pours it overboard.

'You guys can wait in the hull,' he says. 'We'll tell you to suit up when a shark arrives.'

In the hull of the boat, we huddle together shivering.

'Okay boys,' says Wayne, poking his head through the door, 'we have a shark. Who wants to go first?'

Unanimously, we elect Lars.

The great white is about 3 metres long. I've never seen one before and feel a combination of excitement and dread as it circles the boat. The brothers connect a rope from the boat to the cage and then throw the cage overboard. As the cage bobs on the surface a few feet from the boat, they open the top of it and encourage Lars to jump in. This, we realise, is a delicate manoeuvre. The cage is only about a metre wide and if he lands either side of it, he's mincemeat. He jumps from the boat, lands in the cage and Darryl secures it shut. Initially, the shark isn't interested in Lars but when more blood is tipped into the ocean, it throws its tail against the cage. After 20 minutes Lars comes out and is replaced by TJ. When his stint is over, everybody looks at me.

'Come on Aussie,' says Wayne, 'it's time to get you back for the rugby.'

I curse the Australian rugby team. Do they have any idea, as they swan around in high-powered cars with beautiful girls, about the effect they're having on other travelling Aussies?

By the time I hit the water there are three sharks circling, and one is a 5-metre beast. I feel the cold rush of water draining through my wetsuit. I hear a splash and see blood and oil swirling beside me and suddenly realise what's happening—someone is actually tipping blood into the cage with me.

I break the surface to protest and hear a muffled noise through the goggles: 'Mooveeoooorhhaaahh.'

'What?' I shout, taking off my goggles.

'Move your hand!'

I move my hand and the 5-metre shark launches at the cage, clenching its jaw where my hand was one second earlier. As the shark twists its jaws around the cage, I'm thrown from side to side in a death rattle. Only a foot away, I stare at the whites of its eyes, the red gums and the razor teeth. Instinctively, my mind shifts and I view everything from third person—like I'm watching a movie of somebody else. At the moment when I think the poor sod in the cage might be in serious trouble, the shark lets go and disappears. With the sting of cold water comes reality.

'Hey guys,' I shout, raising my head above the surface, 'I think I've had enough.'

'What's wrong Aussie? You've only been in there for five minutes,' yells Wayne.

'Nah seriously, give me a hand out.'

'Orright orright, hold ya horses.'

He thrusts his hand from the side of the boat and I reach up and clutch it.

'Watch out,' he shouts, while pulling me up.

I quickly turn but there are no sharks nearby. They crack up laughing; they really are the kind of people to pull that sort of a joke. I take off the wetsuit, blow my fingers for warmth, and look forward to land.

My map-reading ability needs improvement. Expecting Jeffreys Bay is only a few hours away, I catch a bus from Cape Town in the morning and arrive in Jeffreys at midnight. Apart from being hideously tedious, the trip gives me a chance to make all my usual mistakes, like catching the wrong bus, and then, when I get the right one, leaving all my money behind at a café. (Everyone has to wait as we back-track for 20 minutes. Luckily my wallet is still lying untouched on a table. Every cloud.)

After arriving, I lumber my stuff through the pouring rain to Island Vibe Backpackers. The hostel is shut. I spend ten minutes ringing the doorbell but there's no response — I don't know why I thought there would be. Saturated, I curl up in a ball and fall asleep outside the doorway.

'Looks like you're having a rough night,' I hear, and wake to a beaming torch.

'Yeah,' I reply, still half-asleep. 'I was wondering if there are any rooms available.'

'Sorry bro, can't help,' says the voice, which belongs to a middle-aged South African man. 'I'm not sure if you know, but there's a surfing competition on at the moment and we're fully booked for the weekend.'

'But I don't have anywhere else to go,' I plead.

'Bloody Aussies,' he says, but his voice is light and without malice. 'Follow me, I'll see what I can do.'

I grab my bags and surfboards and follow the man. As we walk around to the back of the hostel, I catch a glimpse of his face. He has blond hair, a moustache and a weathered complexion. His name is Bill and he's the maintenance worker on the property. He opens a sliding glass door and we enter a games room.

'You might be alright here for tonight,' he says, pointing at a couch. 'We should be able to find a bed for you tomorrow.'

I thank him and curl up on the couch but my mind ticks with excitement and I can't sleep. Stumbling around the room in the darkness, I see posters of famous surfers on the walls. Old-style surfboards hang from the ceiling. The hostel is situated above the beach. I open the sliding door and walk outside. I feel the wet grass against my feet and hear a dull thumping noise as the waves crash below. Although unable to see in the dark, I already know it's the best hostel I've ever stayed at.

In the morning, I wake to the smell of bacon and the sound of boisterous laughter. Around a kitchen table backpackers are telling funny stories. Outside it's cloudy but there's a beautiful view along the coast. At a lookout in the backyard, I sit on a well-worn sofa and chat to an old American guy.

'Where's Jeffreys Bay?' I ask.

'It's on the next point of the coast,' he replies. 'If you look from here, you can just see the start of the wave.'

I look along the coast and see the swells running to the next point.

After breakfast I go to the office of the hostel and attempt to check in.

'Well you're in luck boyo,' says Jan, the receptionist, with a smile. 'The only bed we've got available is in a room with five girls. I guess we'll have to squeeze you in there.'

Jan tells me she is going to the surfing competition in five minutes, so I quickly dump my gear on a spare bed and catch a ride while my new room-mates sleep.

Jeffreys Bay is a ten-minute drive from the hostel. Inside the car are two German girls and two English guys. When we arrive, we thank Jan for the lift, walk through a grassy area to a set of wooden steps, and catch our first real glimpse of Jeffreys Bay. Although a strong wind brushes the swells, the potential of the wave is obvious.

The lines of swell sweep in from far out in the ocean, then wrap around the headland as they pick up in speed and power. It's an incredibly long wave. If you were to pick off the right wave and not wipe-out, I guess you could easily ride it for 800 metres.

Along the shoreline are 30 people and near a tower where the surfers change, there's a small stand with about 20 kids. Most wear hooded jumpers and clutch their hands in their pockets to keep warm. Even with all the hype in surfing magazines, Jeffreys has remained a country town.

It's amazing to think that the best surfers in the world are in one of the most famous competitions in the world—and there are only 50 people watching.

The first heat of the contest is between Mick Fanning, Troy Brooks and a surfer I don't recognise. During the heat, Brooks, after speeding across the wall of a wave, grabs his rail at full speed and does a cutback that's so long, drawn-out and beautiful a chorus of 'Aahhh' comes from the kids in the stand. At surfing contests I've heard similar crowd support for aerials and tubes—but never for a cutback. A realisation hits: I could have surfed since the age of two, have the best boards in the world, be fit and agile, have thousands of dollars in sponsorship, and still never be able to pull off such a move.

Brooks actually loses the heat to Mick Fanning. This, I realise, highlights the problem with professional surfing. The heats on the WCT are 30 minutes long and the judges score each wave out of 10. Having checked on the internet, I know the judging criteria is to reward points for doing the most critical manoeuvre in the most critical part of the wave. But I still think the system is flawed. Even with this judging system, Fanning can comfortably rack up four or five snaps down the line for a 7 and Brooks can pull off the cutback of a lifetime for a 5.

When the wind swings offshore, the swell lines straighten and push fast tubes along the point. With the improved conditions, the surfing goes from fun to amazing. Andy Irons scores a 10, Joel Parkinson scores a 10, and

Danny Wills free-falls into a beast and only gets a 9.5. On the beach I catch a glimpse of the mohawked 18-year-old Brazilian prodigy Adriano de Souza, who won the WQS tour last year. Strangely, Kelly Slater does not show for his heat (rumour has it he's still on a golf course in Port Elizabeth).

It takes me one whole morning to fall in love with Jeffreys Bay. I love the way young kids hang with their dads and ask questions about Kelly Slater. I love how their dads respond with guarded enthusiasm. I love that while a quarter of the spectators wear surf-brand clothes, three-quarters don't. I love how you can buy the best homemade shepherd's pie I've ever tasted from a friendly old lady near the competition site, and warm yourself as you eat it. I love the misty rain. I love the South African girls, who rug up in jumpers and don't cast sideways glances at professional surfers.

Back at the hostel I meet my room-mates, who are 18-year-old girls content to laugh at my lame jokes and use me as a sounding board for advice on guys. I tell them we are simple creatures. They seem impressed with a little trick I let them in on, which is to repeat the last word of every sentence to the guy they're talking with, then nod their head and smile, thus giving the guy a chance to do what he really likes, which is to keep talking about himself.

Later, a fancy dress party is thrown in the bar of the hostel and we all get blind drunk on toxic liqueurs. We then go into town to a party for the surfing competition. Incredibly, there's a band I recognise from Western Australia playing, so of course I drunkenly brag about knowing them to anyone that'll listen. I must have looked quite silly wearing a sheet (all I could find at short notice for the fancy dress) and shouting requests 3 feet from the stage but the South Africans happily throw me into the drunken patriotic category.

In the morning I wake with a pounding headache.

'Looks like a good remedy,' says a girl sitting beside me in the communal kitchen, pointing at my coffee and eggs on toast.

'Yeah, I'm giving up alcohol,' I tell her.

The girl's name is Kristen. She's a vet from America who's doing a six-month stint studying animals in Africa. She seems like the outgoing type so when I suggest we go surfing, she happily agrees.

We surf a small beach break in front of the hostel. In the waves, we get to know each other. She grew up in Maryland, a state on the east coast of America, has just finished her vet degree, and enjoys competing in triathlons in her spare time. Last year she rode a bicycle from one side of America to the other. I've often wondered about the strange anomalies America regularly throws into the mix. What attractive girl, for example, travels the world by herself and considers a three-month bike ride fun?

'How'd I go on that one?' she asks, after paddling back from catching a wave.

'Not bad,' I respond, not wanting to face the truth.

The truth is she's a natural. It took me a year to learn how to paddle, stand and ride across a wave and she's doing it on her first surf. I block my mind from a scary realisation: Given a few years' practice, her ability may surpass mine.

That night I walk Kristen to a Mexican restaurant which is having a low-key after-party for the surfing competition. (Mick Fanning defeated Taj Burrow in the final.) Along the way, after we discover an abandoned basketball court and have fun trying to touch the hoop (I take three attempts and she takes one), she kisses me under a full moon. Feeling aroused and deciding the thought of what she sees in me is too complicated to immediately grapple, with I kiss her back.

At the restaurant she lets me fondle her bum and I feel pretty good with myself, drinking tequila and pointing out famous surfers. Back at the hostel I convince her to sleep beside me on a bed 3 feet wide, next to mascara lids, hairdryers and discarded pink pyjamas.

In the morning, as the 18-year-old girls drop more make-up to the floor, we lie in bed feeling embarrassed and discuss our plans for the day. Kristen has two weeks to make it to Durban for work and plans to catch a bus in the afternoon. It takes me 40 minutes to encourage her to miss the bus, which has already been paid for, and travel with me. We make a rough plan—I still have two weeks before my departing flight from Durban so we decide to catch a taxi to the bus station in Jeffreys Bay, catch a bus to Port Elizabeth, and then book a hire car and head up the coast to Durban.

'Not you again,' sighs the taxi driver, when he pulls up beside the hostel.

He's a middle-aged man I've never seen before.

'Have we met?' I ask.

'I gave you a lift home two nights ago—you were swaying in the middle of the road, wearing a sheet.'

'I can't remember that.'

'No,' he replies with a chuckle, 'I didn't think you would.'

Kristen gives me what will soon become a regular look—a mixture of bemusement and concern. Visions of the fancy dress night shuffle through my mind but I draw a blank on getting home.

The taxi drops us at a bus station. Our ride to Port Elizabeth is not a bus but a large van crammed with people. The driver, a young black man, receives us with a toothy grin and spends 20 minutes trying to figure out how to secure my surfboards to the roof. The passengers on board are all black and words from a strange language bounce between them as they help tackle the problem. Eventually the driver gives up on tying the boards to the roof and they're crammed between everybody in the van. At this moment I understand one difference between their culture and ours—for two hours we drive to Port Elizabeth with people squashed against the windows, never complaining about the foolish Westerners and their surfboards.

We hire a car in Port Elizabeth, drive for five hours up the coast and arrive at East London to discover a hotel that has a deal: Book after eight o'clock and it's half price for a room. Happy with our luck and with an hour to spare, we go to a nearby restaurant, drink some cold beers and order a barbecued hog, which Kristen doesn't mind eating even though she's a vet.

'We've got a motto back home,' she tells me. 'If you can't treat it, eat it.' (I'm really starting to fall for the girl.)

That night in the hotel I run a bath and, hoping to come across as devilishly spontaneous, re-create a scene from a movie I've seen where the actor asks the actress for a towel and then pulls her into the bath with him. In the movie the scene ends with the actress laughing and kissing the actor. In the hotel it ends with Kristen calling me mental and demanding that I dry her clothes.

The next day we drive up the coast to Coffee Bay, which is to travellers wanting to find themselves what heroin is to rock stars wanting to lose themselves. Coffee Bay is located on a beach in the middle of nowhere. During the day the waves are flat so there's not much to do except sit around and analyse existential concepts with the backpackers. It's at night, however, that the place comes alive.

After dinner is eaten around a communal table, a pool competition starts. To liven the competition there are various pointless rules to encourage drinking. For example, you must always hold your drink in your left hand and never leave it on the side of the pool table. If this happens, someone will shout 'buffalo' and you immediately have to scull the drink. The situation, I realise, is most dangerous to new people who have no idea of the rules and during my first night I have 'buffalo' called on me so many times it sounds like a continuous echo bouncing from the inside of a cave.

After a few nights of the buffalo games, we leave Coffee Bay and drive for hundreds of miles on gravel tracks past the kind of green hills described in Hemingway novels. Not trusting Kristen with navigation, I take control of the journey and promptly get us lost.

The Kristen situation is bizarre. For starters, she not only agrees to sleep with me but often laughs at my jokes and seems to find my company entertaining. Of course, if I'm comfortable within myself I would take all this as a blessing but instead I do what I always do with girls I like, which is to constantly annoy them.

Eventually we make it to Durban and return the hire car with surprisingly little damage—only a shredded tyre. At the airport I feel sad swapping email addresses with Kristen. She really is an amazing girl but I know, deep in my heart, that she's destined for a suave American doctor and my position as travelling boyfriend is only a substitute role.

At an internet café in the departure lounge, I read a remarkable email from Dad—I have actually climbed the ranking on the WQS. I check the ASP website with excitement. Although I didn't make it on time to my heat in Durban, points were awarded to me for entering and because it's a 6-star contest (meaning that the competition had a high amount of ratings points allocated to it), I'm now ranked 845th—ahead of eight other surfers on the tour. With renewed vigour, I buy a surfing magazine and board my plane to England.

Re: NEWQUAY entry
From: Brodie
Sent: Tuesday, 11 July 2006 8:33:27 AM
To: Sullivan McLeod

Hi Sullivan,

Great to hear that you are getting back in the water, I have entered you into the 5 star Rip Curl Board Masters – Newquay. As per the 2006 ASP calendar you are a late entry as the deadline for the event was on the 30th of June.

Thanks,

James
In office for Brodie until 27th of July
ASP Australasia Administration
Surfing Australia

Newquay, July

I arrive at Heathrow, the busiest airport in Europe, on a rainy day. Although it's the middle of summer in England, this does not surprise me. From previous visits I know the weather in Britain is about as reliable as the midnight train to Tuscany. On the tube from Heathrow I discover what's left of politeness on English public transport has eroded with the terrorist attacks.

England is the one of the few countries in Europe that does not consider surfing a novelty. On the train people trip on my board bag, no doubt unimpressed with my decision to bring it on the train. As people jam up the aisle, I'm pinned against the window, my face pressed against the bulky board bag, which is stuffed with the three boards I bought in Indonesia.

I get off at Bethnal Green Station and drag the board bag past a tattered pub. Having visited my brother before, I've found I like the ramshackle buildings, small corner stores and old pubs of Bethnal Green. There's honesty to the cockney types and immigrants who live here. I buy two pairs of socks for a pound from an enthusiastic street seller, walk past a pub where an old man is propping himself up against the bar, possibly dreaming of a better life, and walk through an alleyway following my memory of where my brother lives.

At my brother's house, I knock on the door but no one's home. My 27-year-old brother, Ash, is an English teacher at the local school. I yell for a few minutes, then dump my gear in his backyard and go searching for a little shop that I remember sells tasty bagels for a pound. After going back to my brother's and discovering there's still no one home, I curl up and fall asleep in his garden.

'You wanna come in mate?' I hear.

In the darkness, I brush the leaves from my shirt and enter the house. It's my brother's flatmate Lee. Lee is in his mid-20s and is also a schoolteacher.

'Wanna cup of tea?' he asks.

'Thanks,' I reply. 'Weren't you a bit surprised that someone was asleep in your backyard?'

'Not really,' he says, fetching two mugs from the cupboard. 'After all, that's where we found you last time.'

Thinking back a year I realise he's right. I'd just arrived from Norway, gone on a bender with a friend, and had fallen asleep in their garden.

'Sorry about never calling ahead,' I say, sipping the tea.

'That's alright mate,' he says. 'To be honest, it'd be a shock if you did.'

We laugh together—I've almost forgotten about English wit.

'So where's Ash anyway?' I ask.

'Haven't you heard?'

'No.'

'He's in hospital with dengue fever.'

Lee informs me that it's a virus similar to malaria which Ash has contracted while on holidays in Thailand.

'Don't worry, he's okay. Actually, he should be out tomorrow.'

Feeling guilty about my ignorance, I thank Lee, have a shower and crash out on my brother's floor.

Ash arrives the next morning. He's still weak from the fever but is in good spirits and I cheer him up with tales of my trip so far. I ask him if he wants to catch a train with me to Newquay (a town four hours south-west of London) for the next surfing competition, but he needs the rest and declines. Knowing the chances of cheap accommodation will be bleak in Newquay, he lends me his tent and snaps a photo of me leaving the house. It's a funny sight—the tent is tightly packed with my three surfboards inside my board bag, and my backpack hangs around my shoulders.

While going down an escalator at Kings Cross Station, my board bag bursts open and the steel pins of the tent scatter everywhere. As the pins jam the escalator, the clockwork of people catching trains quickly turns into chaos. I gather the pins and stuff the tent inside the next bin I come across.

I nearly die of shock when discovering the price of a train from London to Newquay (£70 one way). As the Brits would say, you're havin' a laugh. Still, there's no cheaper option on short notice so I pay the fare to the poker-faced attendant and jump on board. It's a Friday afternoon so for the first few hours the train is packed with workers going home from London. When it empties, I sit on a vacant seat.

'Scuse me, do ya mind if we sit down next to ya?' I hear, and look up to see two smiling teenagers.

I tell them I don't mind and move my board bag from the seat beside me. Both have torn black jeans, black shirts and facial piercing. They introduce themselves as Ritz and Daniel. From the inside of a black bag they produce two beers.

'Wanna drink mate?'

'Thanks,' I reply, and take a sip of the warm beer.

They tell me their story. They've come from Colchester to take a break from studying A-levels. Their plans are loose—they'll go back to Colchester when the money runs out. They both possess the right kind of humour; their jokes are more inclusive than exclusive. They are real. They are the type of teenagers I always wanted to be.

'So where are you going to stay?' Daniel asks me when we arrive in Newquay and dismount the train.

'I haven't really thought about it.'

'We're goin' campin'. Do you wanna come with us?'

I agree. Not because I have no other options but because they remind me of an innocence I've lost and want back. Behind their tattered shirts is an excitement to discover the world, and I've forgotten that feeling.

As we walk towards the camping ground I look at the surf shops and pubs and realise that Newquay, once a quaint seaside town, has first been strangled by the concept of surfing, and then by the concept of bucks' nights. Outside one pub a man wearing goggles, flippers and a snorkel lies unconscious on the footpath. What's incredible is not that a man has drunkenly passed out wearing scuba gear at five in the afternoon, but that nobody has noticed. After checking his snorkel to discover he's still breathing, I drag my board bag around him.

The campsite is further than we guess. When asking for directions we receive varied responses. Eventually we find it about a kilometre from town. Not wanting to pay, we walk past the entrance then hike our gear over a fence and run through the ground with glee.

The caravan park is unlike anything I've seen. It's a massive field crammed with people. Everyone is young and pale. Most have shaved heads, tattoos and drink beer while listening to loud music from hotted-up cars.

'Bloody chavs,' says Daniel, sipping a beer and surveying the scene.

He explains to me the acronym of the slang—council

housed associated vermin. I have the impression he does not easily gel with them.

After erecting their tent, Daniel and Ritz steal a tag from another tent (which you need to prove you've paid) and clip it to their own.

'Where are you gonna sleep?' Daniel asks me.

'Dunno,' I reply, reflecting that ditching my tent in London may have been a tad hasty.

'You can sleep inside our tent if ya want, it'll be bloody cold otherwise.'

At the caravan park store we pool our money, buy a crate of beer and drink it during the night. At midnight the teenagers squash into the tent. I stash my surfboards behind the tent and then join them inside, sleeping on the empty board bag. We're all only a few inches apart but they're not self-conscious and soon begin snoring, oblivious to the continual music outside.

When I wake the next morning I grab the 6'4" square-tail and catch a bus to the competition site, Fistral Beach, to check the surf. The waves are not spectacular but there are a few small peaks and about 30 surfers out. On the beach, it's a frenzy of activity; temporary buildings are being erected in preparation for the contest, which is due to start in a few days. Some of the locals are quite good surfers. I catch a few small waves but have one of those frustrating surfs where my feet are always in the wrong position on the board.

After an hour I go in and walk to the contest site, hoping

to confirm my place in the competition. I speak to Mark, an organiser of the event, who checks the list of entrants and discovers I'm not on it.

'Don't worry, just come here Monday morning. I'm sure we'll be able to find a place for ya,' he says with a smile.

His pleasant demeanour takes me by surprise. I received the same polite manner when talking to the contest officials in South Africa. A scary realisation hits—these people actually think I'm a professional surfer.

The following day I have another practice surf. The swell has picked up slightly and my 6' 4" feels better with the extra push. After the surf, I speak to the contest director.

'You're a late entrant, we'll have to put you in the early rounds,' he informs me, as if my surfing ability might usually warrant a higher entry. (The higher seeded surfers usually start later in the contest. Sometimes the highest ranked surfers do not start the competition until the money rounds; these are the rounds, usually 3 or 4, where the prize money will begin to be allocated.)

'The men's division starts at seven tomorrow morning. It'll be a good idea to come early because you'll be in one of the first heats,' he explains.

A girl smiles and secures a competitor's band to my wrist, then gives me a bag of freebies—a surfing magazine, wax and T-shirt.

'There's a sports scientist that wants to do tests on you guys,' she tells me. 'Do you mind hanging around for a bit?'

Finding it hard to turn down the girl, I agree and she calls out for the scientist, a fit-looking guy in his thirties, who comes bounding into the room.

'Hello mate, are you one of the guys in the comp?'

'Yeah.'

'You don't mind if we run a couple of tests, it's just for a study on the fitness of professional surfers.'

'No worries,' I reply, feeling like my cover as a professional athlete is about to be blown.

We go into another room and the sports scientist requests that I remove my shirt. Although I hold my stomach in, the flab is clearly visible.

'Mmmm,' he says professionally, while scrutinising the excess fat.

'I haven't really been training lately,' I confess.

For an hour he tests my flexibility, lung capacity, skin-fold fat and aerobic ability. When it's over I leave hurriedly.

Back at the campsite, Daniel and Ritz have stolen a case of beer and are on their fifth can. They offer a beer. Resolving that it will help me sleep later, I accept and we begin drinking games. The beer does not help me sleep. I wake during the night with anxious thoughts, wondering how much of a fool I'll make of myself in tomorrow's contest.

In the morning I drag my board bag through the rain and beer rubble. At the campsite bus stop, I discover the bus service does not start for an hour. While cursing and vowing to change my hopeless decisions, I meet a girl and convince her to lend me her phone to call a taxi. The taxi arrives 30 minutes later and whisks me down to the beach. I need not have bothered rushing. Because of strong onshore winds, the ocean is completely blown out and the officials decide to delay the start of the contest for a few hours.

'Doesn't look too good,' I say to an official, as we're pelted with rain.

'Welcome to the QS,' he replies in an American drawl.

There is a competitors' tent on a hill overlooking the beach. I enter the tent and look at the heat schedule, which tells us when we're due to surf and who against. I'm in the second heat of the morning—against another Aussie, Josh Lewan, an Englishman, Sam Smart, and a guy from Portugal, Ruben Gonzalez. It feels weird to see my name neatly typed up on the sheet of paper against the others.

I change into my wetsuit then walk to the check-in area and catch my first glimpse of Josh Lewan. With his curly blond hair and blue eyes he looks like the typical surfer, but his wetsuit gives me hope—it's an old-school brand that's tattered at the hems. Maybe he's also winging it.

I'm assigned a blue contest vest. It feels surreal to collect it from the beach marshal and pull it over my head. Josh Lewan is in a red vest. I walk with him to the water edge and nervously spark a conversation.

'It's a good thing you're up against me,' I tell him. 'I'm not that good.'

'Yeah right,' he replies, looking at me like I'm playing mind games.

'No seriously, I shouldn't be too hard to beat.'

'No worries,' he says, but I can tell he doesn't believe me.

We do stretches on the sand and I wonder why I'm telling him all this. The other competitors keep their distance. With a pounding heart, I brace the surf and begin the paddle through the chop.

As soon as we make it through the whitewater, a massive storm hits. With the rain and wind, it's impossible to hear the siren that will start our heat. I decide to sit beside Josh Lewan and start catching waves when he does.

The conditions are terrible for a surfing competition, the waves are windblown and mostly closing out, but there is the odd rideable peak breaking around us. Josh picks off a fat right. Any notion I have that his surfing ability might be lacking is quickly abolished when he pulls a tight arc before me. Not knowing the time left, I become frantic and paddle for any lump of moving water. I see a wedgy left and turn late, getting clipped by the lip as I jump to my feet. I make the drop but my feet are in the wrong position on the board and I fall on an attempted floater. I gather my 6' 4" square-tail and paddle back out knowing I've just blown a valuable chance to rack up a good score.

Josh comes screaming past on another wave, bouncing

off the sections and carving his board through the water. After a few minutes waiting, I pick off a right. It's a slow wave but I manage a cutback and a small re-entry before it shuts down. Blasted by howling wind, it's impossible to hear the scores but I guess I'm in fourth because Josh already has two good ones and the others have been picking them off further down the beach.

Adriano de Souza, the mohawked Brazilian, paddles past me for the next heat. It's the closest I've been to de Souza and I feel like saying something but every sinew of his energy is harnessed for the paddle and his eyes are focused on the line-up. My last wave is a right which breaks too fast to make it around the whitewater. I straighten out and come in.

I sit on the sand for a few moments with a pounding heart, being pelted by the wind and rain. I think back through my heat, analysing where I went wrong and coming to the conclusion that I'm trying too hard. Glancing around, I feel thankful there are no spectators on the beach—although a deserted beach is not how I remember my dreams of competing in a professional surfing competition. Feeling too embarrassed to go back immediately through the competitors' area, I sit on the sand for a few moments being drenched in rain and wondering how many people saw my lame attempt at surfing on the internet.

Eventually, I climb up the dunes and hand over my blue vest to an official. I have visions of him taking me aside and suggesting that I quit competitions but instead he just smiles and says: 'Bloody awful out there.'

In the competitors' area I change from my wetsuit and rest my 6' 4" square-tail, the only sticker-less board in the rack, on a railing. (Stickers on the pro's boards are there to promote sponsors.) The results of our heat are posted in the competitors' tent. I've finished last. As it turns out, no one is awarded high scores but Josh Lewan and the Portuguese surfer, Ruben Gonzalez, make it through.

In the competitors' tent there is a fridge full of Red Bull drinks and two masseurs. I crack open a drink and ask for a massage. A middle-aged man invites me to stretch out on a soft table and begins rubbing my back and shoulders. Adriano de Souza enters the tent, peels off his wetsuit and approaches another masseuse—a friendly looking lady.

'Good morning, do you think it will be possible to have a massage?' he asks politely in crystal-clear English.

'Of course,' she replies, slightly blushing.

With his brown skin and cheeky smile, nobody is immune to his charm.

It's the perfect time to spark a conversation—we are only a metre apart. I spend a few minutes trying to think of an opening sentence and, eventually, go for the most obvious.

'How'd ya go?' I ask, as casually as I can.

He turns and looks at me while the lady kneads his back.

'Good,' he says with a smile. 'I got lucky.'

I really want to ask another question but my mind goes blank, so we both just lie silently, feeling the kneading of pressure against our skin, and I watch other competitors enter the tent.

After the massage I grab my board and make for the bus stop.

'Hey man?' I hear, and turn to see a young American surfer I'd met years ago in a bar in Margaret River. 'You don't remember me, do ya?'

'I do,' I reply, 'but I can't remember your name, what is it again?'

'Bobby.'

I shake his hand and introduce myself again. Bobby is five years younger than me, has blond hair and a stocky build, and is a competitor on the WQS. He introduces me to another American called Chris. Having just arrived, they ask about a place to stay and I mention the caravan park. They offer a lift and I graciously accept and squash my board into their hire car.

'You gotta be kiddin' me,' says Bobby, when we arrive at the caravan park and he negotiates his way through the beer bottles.

'It's not as bad as you think,' I say.

Having yet to surf in the competition, they decide to go somewhere quieter for a good night's sleep. I ask if I can come with them, gather what gear I can find from the campsite, leave a note for Daniel and Ritz, and we drive to a quaint little bed and breakfast. It's a well-kept house with a rose bush outside. We ask the owner, an old lady, about the price of a room. She decides to charge us £18 a night each (which is surprisingly cheap) and we book for three nights. Inside, the house is decorated with pristine cutlery and pre-war looking furniture.

'Why are you over here?' the old lady asks us.

'We're in the surfing comp,' Bobby replies—a response that does not ease her furrowed brow.

I wonder how long it'll take us to get kicked out; she already seems suspicious.

I share a room with Bobby. He unpacks folded clothes into a wardrobe. I look enviously at his quiver of boards—a 6'1", 6'3", 6'4" and 6'10". They're all matching yellow, beautifully shaped, light and covered with sponsors' stickers. I keep my three Indo-shapes in the board bag. After watching a Kelly Slater documentary on his laptop, we go to bed.

In the morning we wake early and drive to the contest site. Chris is in the second heat of the day. He's a talented goofy-footer but fails to catch the right waves and finishes third. In the afternoon, Bobby controls his heat with three nice rights and advances through to the money rounds.

I spend the day with the affable Americans. Their demeanour is more serious than Australians and they have a different sense of humour but there's something I like about them—they don't judge. I'm surprised at the ease with which they've accepted me, a less competent surfer, into their group. They are both good-looking clean-cut types but, after scratching the surface, I realise they're an odd pairing. Although both are raised on the west coast of California, Bobby in Santa Barbara and Chris in San Diego, Bobby survives solely on surfing prize money while Chris is also a professional gambler. Once again I wonder about America—how is it possible to churn out a shy kid who travels the world surfing and playing poker?

The following morning, after toast and orange juice with our landlady, we go to the contest site to discover Bobby has drawn the hardest heat of the day. It's against a well-known Aussie, Travis Lynch, and two Brazilians, William Cardoso and Heitor Alves. The heat is run on a low tide in shifty one-footers. During the heat I discover a fact that will re-occur during the week—no one grovels as well as the Brazilians. As soon it begins they both rack up scores of 9.

Bobby comes in dejected but in my opinion he does well to finish third. Travis Lynch, the more fancied surfer, is so comprehensively beaten that with a minute to go he needs two high-scoring rides just to reach Bobby.

Having finished in the first money round, Bobby collects his prize money (eight American 100-dollar notes in an envelope), and I convince him to have a beer with me. We drink beers in an up-market bar that overlooks the sun setting above the windblown ocean. After he's drunk enough to loosen up, I take the opportunity to ask all the questions I've always wanted to know about professional surfing. Who are the nice guys? Who are the bastards? What tactics are used to win?

To my surprise he replies with startling honesty. He tells me the names of surfers who hassle. He mentions the name of a Hawaiian surfer who has physically threatened him. It feels like I've cracked the professional surfing world. Sitting in the bar, I feel the urge to remember the setting sun and the taste of the beer. I want to remember everything he says but most importantly, I want to remember why I feel warm talking to him — because for the first time on the tour I feel included.

After finishing the beer we walk along the beach. It's a blistering cold night. In town, chaos spreads like a wild germ harvested in a bad crop. I've clearly underestimated Newquay as the buck/hens' night capital of England. On the main street there are girls wearing wedding dresses pinned with condoms and lollypops and a group of lads pushing a man wearing a monkey suit in a cage with 'the Gimp' written across it.

We enter a packed bar. Inside, the surfers who have been knocked out of the contest are drinking and dancing. Near the dance floor, the Brazilians puff out their chests and scope for girls. The Aussies hang in a group near the bar. Most are tall and blonde, wear cheesy grins, blue jeans and white shoes.

I buy two shots and we scull them down. Then Bobby buys two more and soon we're both drunk. Feeling loose and foolhardy, we meet two girls and try all the usual drunk schmoozer moves. The girls are called Sarah and Felicity and have come down from London to check out the surfing competition. When they ask Bobby what he's doing in Newquay, he replies that he's just travelling around. Once again I'm impressed with his lack of ego—it's the perfect opportunity to mention being a competitor. We dance with the girls for a few hours and then catch a taxi with them back to our bed and breakfast accommodation.

'Shhh, keep quiet,' Bobby whispers as we enter. 'The chick running this place is a Nazi.'

The girls laugh and mock his American accent. Inside, it's quickly apparent that no one will be getting any action with the sleeping arrangements (two single beds a metre apart), so Bobby and Sarah go to the bathroom. I lie on the bed with Felicity, trying to control a spinning room. Feeling a convoluted haze around my brain, I kiss her and we fumble to take off our clothes.

Suddenly there's a shriek from next door. Bobby and Sarah come into the room, wrapped in towels; they've been caught by the landlady.

'How dare you bring uninvited guests back here,' she scolds.

I quickly pull up my pants and throw the blanket over us.

'Who's under here?' she demands, pulling back the blanket.

The sight that greets her fails to please.

Initially, she demands that we leave immediately but

after our pleading she agrees to kick us out first thing in the morning. We call a taxi for the girls, who seem more amused than embarrassed, and say goodbye. Back in the room, we scull water and clean up.

'Don't suppose it's worth asking for breakfast tomorrow,' Bobby adds, and we go to bed laughing.

We wake early in the morning and leave. Chris, who'd gone to bed early the previous night, is not impressed with our antics.

'Where are we gonna go now?' he grumbles, as we drive through the town.

Having both been knocked out of the competition, they decide to drive back to London. They drop me off at the caravan park. I say goodbye and swap email addresses with Bobby, who plans to compete in the rest of the European events.

I dump my surfboards behind Daniel and Ritz's tent and then walk to the competition site, which is packed with people. The finals of the surfing contest are run alongside a skateboarding competition. I bump into Josh Lewan beside the skateboarding half-pipe.

'Are you still in the surf comp?' I ask.

'Nah, I got knocked yesterday. I'm entering the skate-boarding competition.'

'Really? Are you any good?'

'I dunno, we'll see,' he says with a grin.

Along with the blond hair, hat and earphones, he also sports a fake diamond earring which looks ridiculous.

'Nice earring,' I say.

'Thanks,' he replies.

'What are you listening to?'

'My song. Here, see what you think.'

He takes off the earphones and puts them on my head. A deep voice beams through the speakers. Although it sounds like the kind of commercial R&B that's constantly played these days on radio, it's a catchy tune.

'Is that really you?' I ask, handing him back the headphones.

'Yeah, I have to go back to Australia in a few weeks because Universal has just bought the song off me. Anyway, I'm running late for the skate comp, I'll catch ya.'

I watch him leave. He really is an unbelievable character—a professional surfer travelling the world as an aspiring pop star.

The Newquay competition is a farce. It's well-known to everyone, even people who don't surf, that the west coast of England receives few swells in summer. There are waves in winter but fewer tourists. This is the conundrum for organisers: Hold the event when there are waves but no spectators, or spectators but no waves. For the main sponsor, Rip Curl, it's an easy decision. If no one is on the beach, no one will see the banners and no one will buy the clothes that make the profit. Therefore, each year people swarm down to Newquay, no doubt bemused to see professional surfers, who have flown in from all corners of the globe, pump across knee-high waves. In its purest form the decision to hold the competition in August is a direct analogy of commercial needs overpowering commonsense.

Despite the woeful conditions, Adriano de Souza surfs amazingly well; he can somehow maintain speed through the small waves and lands airs comfortably. Although he's a late entry and required to surf from the first round, throughout the event he looks unstoppable. The only surfer who seems capable of beating him is another Brazilian, Heitor Alves, a flashy goofy-footer who's light on his feet and also quick in the small surf. Remarkably, both Brazilians are knocked out in the semi-finals; de Souza because he panics and chooses the wrong waves, and Alves because he gets penalised for interference (a dubious decision by the judges who deem that he's blocked the other surfer).

In a tent reserved for competitors I watch the final (between an Aussie, Cory Ziems, and a South African, David Weare) with the rest of the surfers. They are an unruly mob and lie shirtless on a couch, talking amongst themselves and speculating on the judges' scores on waves. I sit next to two South Africans, Jordy Smith and Damien Fahrenfort. I remember watching Fahrenfort carve up the waves in Durban. He's tall, blond, charismatic and annoys the hell out of me. His confident swagger reminds me of a kid I went to school with, who the teachers admired, the girls loved and the boys sucked up to. Of course, if I face the truth, the assessment is only spawned by jealousy.

David Weare wins the final. I watch Fahrenfort and Smith join the rest of the South Africans, who hoist Weare above their shoulders and carry him up the beach. Amongst thousands of spectators, Weare is presented with a check for US $10 000. Weare, a low-ranked WCT competitor, is older than most of the other professionals and speaks eloquently, thanking the sponsors and his fiancée.

After the competition, an exclusive dance party is held inside a massive tent on the beach. Apparently there's a famous DJ who'll perform to a select few sponsors, event organisers and VIPs. While waiting in a queue outside the tent, I encounter the perks of professional surfing. A security guard recognises me from being tested by the sports scientist and shouts: 'Let him through, he's one of the competitors.'

A path is cleared and I walk through the onlookers feeling both foolish and proud.

Inside, the atmosphere is stale. People are scattered around in small groups and the DJ plays well-known covers. I scam as many free drinks as possible and then walk into town, which heaves with drunk girls and pouting surfers.

I trawl through a few pubs where the surfers hang out, sculling beers and analysing the pro surfing circus through drunken eyes, then stumble towards the Walkabout—an Aussie pub-chain which, when sober, I swore I'd never go into. Inside they're playing feel-good 1980s songs. I meet a girl at the bar. She's tall, has red hair and looks in her early thirties. The girl has a good sense of humour and a carefree way about her but I have the impression that neither of us would be attracted to the other if sober. After stumbling around the dance floor, we sit down on a couch in a quiet part of the pub. We kiss—light talk is not needed.

'Get it out,' she says, fondling my pants.

She really is that forward.

'Not here,' I reply.

'Why not?'

'There's cameras.'

We walk outside to a beach, which is illuminated by two massive spotlights, and see couples rolling around on the sand. The idea that the lights will deter dodgy behaviour does not appear to be working. We walk past the couples, past a cliff and drop on the sand. The girl swiftly produces a condom from her purse and puts it in my hand. As she pulls down my pants I realise that I still don't know her name.

Suddenly, a wave rolls up the sand and drenches us. We laugh and pull up our clothes. The cold water acts as a reminder. We are not movie stars in the heat of passion but drunk strangers. As we walk back up the beach, I brush sand from my shirt and hear the slish-slosh of wet shoes.

'Are you hungry?' I ask.

'Not really,' she replies.

Her demeanour has changed since the beach incident. She seems less confident and more embarrassed.

'I'll just be two seconds,' I tell her, and walk inside a kebab shop full of loud drunk people.

After collecting the kebab, I turn around to discover that she's disappeared. I walk up and down the pavement but there's no sight of her.

I catch a bus back to the caravan park. Ritz and Daniel, the rebellious teenagers, stumble out of their tent smiling.

'Sull, where the hell have ya been?'

They welcome me back like I knew they would, introduce me to their friends, young university students who have just arrived from London, and we drink shots of tequila until sunrise.

In the morning Daniel and Ritz leave, hell-bent on making it back to Colchester before their parents have a 'spack attack'. They ask if I'm coming but I feel too hungover to move. They scrawl their email addresses on a piece of paper and leave their tent for me. I say goodbye and vow to keep in touch. All day, I lie inside the tent feeling like I'm about to die. I'm dehydrated enough to crave water but too paranoid to walk outside and get it. Eventually I muster the courage to leave the tent, walk past groups of guys wearing tracksuit pants and cooking sausages, and buy myself a bacon and egg roll and a bottle of water from a nearby shop. I tell myself I'll never drink again but it feels like a hollow promise.

The next day I feel better. I leave the tent where it is, gather up my smelly clothes, stuff my three surfboards into the board bag and catch a train back to London. My brother has recovered from dengue fever. Over a cup of coffee, I tell him about my week in Newquay, then check the ASP website on his computer.

Incredibly, I've gone up the WQS rankings again. Although I was knocked out in my first heat in Newquay, I'm still awarded 200 points (an amount usually received when advancing through two or three rounds) because there were fewer surfers in the contest. Feeling astonished I look at my name on the ratings list. I've gone up 120 places. I'm now ranked 696 on the WQS — higher than 132 other surfers.

Re: Entry payments
From: Brodie
Sent: Monday, 31 July 2006 8:25:41 AM
To: Sullivan McLeod

Hi Sully,

I can do a late entry for you for the Lacanau Pro if you like, however the alternate list already has 33 guys on it.

Kind regards,

BJC
ASP Australasia Administration
Surfing Australia

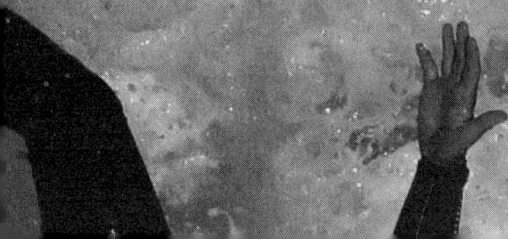

Lacanau, August

Has the world gone crazy? This is the theme of conversation with commuters on a train ride back from Luton Airport (an hour from London). The reason I'm on the train is easily explained; my flight from England to France is cancelled because all planes have been grounded due to a suspected terrorist plot. The reason that I'm in amicable conversation with people on the train, however, has enough twists and nuances to trouble a hemmed-up anthropologist for years.

The truth is I'm scared—and not because of the terrorist alarms. I've been on public transport in London a hundred times and have never seen strangers talk. Isn't there a law forbidding it? After my first ride on a London tube, when I'd asked a girl for the time and she'd looked at me like I'd just burnt down a psychiatric ward, I'd assumed there must be.

Is the shock of a plane exploding into the night sky really enough to start conversing with someone unacquainted? Maybe the inconvenience of having to reshuffle that time-share in Rhodes, having to cancel the hire car (which will not be reimbursed, for Christ's sake), is cause for a grumble. When an old lady enquires happily about my board bag, I realise things are really getting weird. She offers me a place to stay and I panic and jump off the train. Reflecting on the situation, it's possibly an overreaction. I drink some water, catch the next train to Bethnal Green and lug my gear back to my brother's house.

I get drunk with my brother for three days—not the ideal preparation for a surfing contest in France but I've mostly given up on ideals. Back at the airport, this time there's little trouble except for the 400-metre queue to the ticket counter, the assurances from baggage handlers that my boards will not make it, and the sprint to the plane in socks (my shoes have to be removed at the final checkpoint.)

When arriving in Bordeaux we all give a pre-emptive sigh. There's only one thing worse than negotiating customs, querying lost luggage and finding a way into the city, and that's attempting it in French.

'Good news,' a lady tells me at the baggage collection. 'Your surfboards arrived.'

'Oh thanks.'

'Unfortunately,' she continues, 'the rest of your luggage has not.'

I spend a few moments verbally hypothesising how a 7-foot board bag containing three surfboards, a wetsuit and an old sleeping bag (which my brother has lent me) could make it on board before a standard backpack.

'I'm wearing the only clothes I have. What should I do?' I ask her.

I don't know,' she replies airily, in a way that I'll soon find familiar among middle-aged French women. 'Perhaps you can come back tomorrow.'

It has taken her less than a minute to become indifferent towards my deer-in-the-headlights act.

My backpack arrives five hours later. It's handed to me at the airport foyer without an explanation. Leaving the airport in a huff, I drag my gear towards a bus which takes me into the city.

At Bordeaux Central Train Station, it's quickly apparent that I should speak French or at least pretend to. Of course, I should know all this from my last time in France when I'd failed to pin all hopes on the word *bonjour*.

After a lot of confusion, the good-looking yet pissed-off girl behind the counter gives me a ticket to Lacanau, the venue for the surfing competition. A competition that I'm late for but still not sure if I'm competing in. I fall asleep on the train and wake to a conductor speaking a strange set of noises (French).

I walk through Lacanau feeling tired, reflecting that three days of partying with my brother was a bad idea. Needing a cheap place to stay, I approach a small hotel.

The owner not only informs me that it is full but 'et is not pozz-able to find a place to stay ere en sum-mer'.

After two hours spent dragging my board bag and backpack along the street, I discover he's right. At an internet café, I dump my gear and attempt to use a computer, which is possible provided that I can read French.

'Scuse em mwha?' I say to a man behind the counter.

He rushes over with a furrowed brow.

'Is it possible to change the graphics of the computer into English?'

He speaks little English but is friendly and spends 20 minutes trying to fix the problem. It doesn't work. The graphics stay in French. I feel tired, hungry and lost. My hope is that the man will take sympathy on me and offer a place to stay.

'Are you a surf-er?' he asks, noticing my board bag.

'Yes, I'm looking for a place to stay.'

'Yes, but why come ere to surf?'

'I've come for the surfing competition.'

'But sir,' he says with a polite smile, 'zer is no surf ere.'

'Oh, I thought there was a surfing competition, the Lacanau Pro.'

'Yes, zis is true.'

'Then what's wrong?'

'Zis is not Lacanau.'

On the computer before us, he proves that I am, in fact, not in Lacanau but Biscarrosse-plage, a town an hour down the coast. The flighty girl at the train station had obviously lost her patience and sent me in the wrong direction. If I had enough energy to huff, I would, but instead I grab my gear and wander aimlessly through the town.

Eventually I end up on a beach which is in the middle of a massive celebration. There is jazz music and people dressed in strange outfits, cheering on the musicians. Like a zombie, my tired legs drag my board bag and backpack past the chaos.

At a fast-food takeaway on the beach, I join a queue of people rattling off orders of hamburgers and chips to frantic waiters. When it's my turn, the waiter completely ignores my attempt to order in English. After 20 minutes lurking at the counter, a short man, I guess the manager, says: 'Yez siir, what do you want?'

His tone is clipped and the stare he gives is cold enough to assume that I've just stolen a Picasso painting. I eat my hamburger at a vacant table and ponder what to do next. Assuming it's too late for a train to Lacanau, I decide to sleep on the beach. Walking a safe distance away from the music and mayhem, I plonk my gear down on the sand. I throw my sleeping bag around me and use the board bag as a pillow. My backpack is within arm's distance. As my weary eyelids drop I see a group of people not far off, drinking and shouting in French.

I have my best sleep in months, deep enough to wake refreshed but also, unfortunately, not to be disturbed by thieves. In the morning I discover my backpack, which contains all clothes, money, bank cards and my passport, is gone. I tear up the sand in a frenzy but find nothing.

Essentially I now only have three boards, a wetsuit, a sleeping bag and the clothes I'm wearing. I drag it all to a train station and catch a train back to Bordeaux. On board I'm approached by an inspector. His rushed French could only be about showing a valid ticket. After failing to understand or believe my story about having all bank cards stolen, he writes out a fine. I want to tear it up in his face but, having lost all confidence, just stare blankly out the window.

The train stops in Bordeaux. I disembark and sit on a bench for a few minutes trying to figure out what the hell I'm going to do. I go to a police station. After a few minutes bumbling in English, I fill out a theft claim form and they say that they'll let me know if anything turns up, which seems like a strange promise considering I haven't left a contact address or phone number. Regardless, I thank them and drag my board bag to a bus station.

Harnessing all energy, I approach the driver of the bus to Lacanau. Of course my fumbled explanation to the bus driver doesn't work but a man who speaks fluent English overhears the conversation and explains the situation to the driver in French. Eventually the bus driver gives up and lets me on board.

When the bus departs, I sit beside the man who helped me and thank him. His name is Christophe. He has long

blond hair, wears a multicoloured scarf and looks about 40.
He's a university teacher who has come to Lacanau to make
a documentary for his students. He takes a video camera
from a bag and asks if I mind being in the film. I tell him
I don't and he asks questions about life on the surf tour.

When we arrive in Lacanau, an American lady sitting
on the seat in front of us, turns to me and says: 'I overheard
your story about having money stolen. When I was in
Australia last year we had a similar experience and the
Australians were so nice to us.'

She hands me €50 euros. 'It's all I have on me at the
moment but it's at least enough for a meal.'

I thank her wholeheartedly; it really is an incredibly
kind gesture and I feel like the universe is tipping back in
my favour. As I take my board bag from the bus, Christophe
circles me with his video camera and I have the sense that
I'm really living.

Some teenagers approach Christophe and they
exchange lively French. Then the teenagers turn to
me: 'Excuse me, do you know Jeremy Flores?' (A young
professional French surfer.)

I tell them I don't but their excitement remains
undiminished. They produce some French surfing
magazines and happily thrust them before me.

'They want you to sign them,' Christophe explains. 'I
told them you are in the surfing competition.'

I sign the magazines feeling, not for the first time, like
an impostor and then I drag the tattered board bag with

Christophe past small bakeries and fashion boutiques to the beach.

The competition site is located a few hundred metres away. It's a series of circus-sized tents, a stage and large billboards promoting surf-wear and sunglasses. We walk past a checkpoint, past a wooden walkway, and Christophe translates my situation to an organiser. The organiser speaks rapid-fire French with Christophe and then calls for another man, I guess the competition director, who greets me with a smile.

'You can sleep here,' he says, and points to a couch which folds out into a mattress in the competitors' tent. 'Feel free to use our internet or phone to sort out your problems.'

I thank him and lean my board bag up against a railing. Christophe says goodbye, promising to send me a copy of his documentary. I thank him and take in my surroundings. I'm actually in a small competitors' change room. Outside there are wooden walkways and judging areas and a large recreation area filled with pot plants and couches. There are also free drinks and fruit for competitors which can be ordered from a pleasant girl behind a counter. I sit on a couch, eat an apple, drink a Coke and decide to tackle the problem of stolen gear tomorrow.

At night there is an opening party for a new type of vodka so I indulge in free alcohol and then drop off to sleep in the competitors' tent.

✳

In the morning I wake to Rob Machado (former world number 2 and, after Slater, probably the second most famous surfer on the planet) leaning over me.

'Scuse me buddy,' he says in a laid-back American drawl, 'just need to get my wetsuit.'

He pulls the wetsuit from underneath the mattress I'm lying on, comes back moments later with a red contest vest and disappears towards the beach for the start of his heat. I rub my eyes and wonder if I'm dreaming. Five months after starting this journey, I've somehow arrived broke, smelly and deep in the belly of the professional surfing chasm.

In the competitors' lounge I eat two bowls of Cocoa Pops and then track down the ASP tour rep, a young French man called Gregoire, and tell him my story.

'Are you competing?' he asks briskly.

'I think I'm one of the alternates.' (Alternate surfers are surfers who can compete if a higher ranked surfer pulls out.)

He checks a list of names on a wall.

'What is your name?'

'Sullivan McLeod.'

'Nup, you're not on here.'

Because it is a popular 6-star event and I've left it to the last minute to enter, I've obviously not had a ranking high enough to even make it as an alternate. At that moment, another organiser comes into the tent. I leave quickly and decide not to bother Gregoire again. I desperately need to use a phone and computer to sort out my problems and

Gregoire seems more astute than the others and, now that it's clear I'm not in the contest, has the power to throw me out of the VIP area.

I spend the morning calling the Australian embassy. A replacement passport will not be easy. First, I have to find the money to get to Paris and then I have to come up with $200 for another passport. I call my bank in Australia and cancel my credit card, then get stuck in the usual merry-go-round. They can replace my bank cards free of charge but admit it will take weeks for them to arrive in France.

To clear my head, I leave the competitors' area, walk down onto the beach and watch some of the surfing competition. They're running the second round of the event in small waves under a clear blue sky.

'The next surfers in heat 6,' the commentator announces, 'will be Samba Mann in white, Julian Cuello in blue, Alex Grey in red and Davi de Jesus in yellow.'

I sit up, startled—surely it couldn't be Davi?

The last time I saw Davi de Jesus was four years ago in Margaret River. At the time I was working at a caravan park on the beach. One day, my cousin arrived with some friends and, after checking them in, I visited later with a few beers and a guitar. It was around the time of the Margaret River Masters so next door to my cousin was a caravan full of professional surfers. The group included a French surfer, a young Australian and a Brazilian—Davi de Jesus.

From the moment I saw Davi I liked him. He's about 6' 2", and has square shoulders, taut brown skin and a handsome face. He'd been on the road for five months and talked about missing his younger brother in Brazil. He was eating cold spaghetti from a tin; for some reason that stuck in my mind.

The next day at the Margaret River contest I sat with a group of friends and watched Davi pitted against two Americans and a local surfer. As everyone cheered on the local, I silently hoped Davi would do well and was pleased when he scored a few nice rights and finished second.

A day later the main break was hit with a massive swell. The powerful waves were 12 feet by Hawaiian standards. Having been out in similar conditions, I knew the wave was hard to surf at that size—there's a lot of water moving and you need a thick board just to paddle into the waves. Most of the pros were not prepared. They thought they could paddle into the waves on their wafer-thin boards and struggled. Davi was leading his heat until the last five minutes. He turned and paddled for one in the dying moments, couldn't quite get down it, and was pitched from the top of the wave to the trough. When he made it to the shore, I saw him hobble up the beach, barely able to carry his board.

That night I visited him in his caravan. He was lying on a couch with his arm in a cast. He'd spent $50, the last of his money, to see a doctor who'd diagnosed him with a dislocated shoulder.

'I only had to make it through one more heat to reach the money rounds,' he told me, dejected.

He formed a plan; he was going to get a job grape picking when his shoulder healed, hoping to make enough money to reach the next contest.

The following day I'd planned to leave Margaret River to go to the Comedy Festival in Melbourne and asked Dad if he could help me drop off my car for Davi. The car was a dodgy $400 beast I'd named Betsy but I figured it could at least get him to the vineyards and back. When we went to the caravan park, however, he was gone. And that was the last I saw of him.

On the beach at Lacanau, I catch up with Davi after his heat. He's happy to see me and offers help with my situation but I know he doesn't have much money and tell him I'm okay.

That night there is another party in the VIP area. There are free sandwiches, a bowl of salsa, dips and beer. I eat the sandwiches and drink the beer and start a conversation with two South African surfers called Antonio Bortoletto and Gavin Roberts.

'Where are you living bro?' Gavin asks, sipping a beer.

'Right here.'

'What do you mean?'

'I mean I'm sleeping on a mattress in the competitors' tent.'

He looks at me with disbelief for a few moments, then says 'No way' and chinks my glass.

Considering I'm an impostor, it's probably not a smart move to brag about my digs but I'm tired of lying and the whole deception feels like it's about to unravel regardless. As a band plays on a stage near the VIP area, I drink beer with the South Africans and listen to Antonio complain about being knocked out of the contest.

'I can't fuckin' believe Rob got the score on his last one.'

'Were you in the heat with Rob Machado?' I ask.

'Yeah man,' he says. 'Did you see the judges give him a 6 on his last wave? They just gave it to him because of his name.'

I'd seen the heat earlier and was also surprised. With a minute to go and needing a 6 to advance, Machado had taken off on a small wave and only managed a few manoeuvres. Normally, the score would only be 3 or 4 but it'd come through at 6.5.

After watching the band we go to a house with more South Africans, who are blind drunk from sculling tequila. Then we go to a nightclub and I spend 20 of the €50 the friendly lady on the bus had given me.

In the morning I wake to the commentator loudly chastising a bodyboarder for surfing in the competition area. I'd met the surfing commentator the day before; he's a brash American who moulds well to the gig of calling the waves for the spectators. He can speak fluent French but most of his jokes on the bodyboarder are in English, as if to appeal to the other pros.

During the morning, in a caravan used by competition officials, I go through the usual battle of trying to call my bank and the Australian embassy. I form a plan: I'll transfer money from my account into someone else's via the internet, and they can withdraw the money. After approaching some competitors with this haphazard proposal, a friendly young Canadian surfer agrees to help.

When accessing my bank account on the internet, I realise that I only have $3000 of the $20 000 left. In desperation, I sit on some wooden steps and do some quick calculations. Have I really spent that much in South Africa and England? Or did the thieves spend some of it before I cancelled my credit card?

We try to transfer the money but it doesn't work. I call the bank. For some reason they can't tell me if my stolen credit card has been used and offer a complicated set of instructions on transferring money, telling me that it will only work if I transfer the money into an Australian account.

Later that night, in an act of desperation, I approach Nathan Hedge, an Australian pro I've seen in magazines, and two other surfers. I tell them my story and ask if I can transfer money into one of their accounts but they appear sceptical.

'I only need enough to catch a train to Paris to replace my passport,' I say.

'Hang on a second mate,' Hedge replies. 'We don't even know ya.'

I introduce myself to them. Alongside Hedge, there's Matt Griggs, the Rip Curl team manager, and a young surfer called Matt Wilkinson.

'Look, I don't know mate,' Griggs says. 'Maybe it'd be better if you asked someone else.'

Damn self-righteous Aussies. I leave wondering why I approached them in the first place.

In the morning I wake to the berating voice of the commentator hassling out another French surfer for being in the line-up. A perky young French girl comes into the tent.

'Excuse me Sullivan,' she says, 'we have your father on the phone.'

'Pardon?' I reply, to check that I'm not hearing things.

'Your father is on the phone. We got in touch with him last night. We got his number from the details on your contest registration. I hope you don't mind.'

Considering I'm an adult, getting in touch with my father is a strange gesture from the French but I have to give them credit for caring.

I speak to Dad for 20 minutes. He offers to put enough money into my account to make it to Paris but I thank him and say not to worry, realising that even if the money is sent I still don't have a bank card to access it.

I walk outside, past people who line the beach watching the competition, sit down on a rock, write some plans on a notepad and feel utterly hopeless. I have not had a shower for four days. I have worn the same smelly shirt, shorts and shoes. I have €24 to my name, no passport, and no prospects. I'm an outsider to the world of professional surfing. I don't want to hang around the pros. I don't want to enter another competition and get knocked out in the first round. Tears well in my eyes. I'm going to cut short this whole ridiculous trip and go back to Australia. It would be okay if this feeling of hopelessness was new, but it's not. I'm getting used to it—being broke, destitute, homeless, in a country that doesn't speak English. Why don't I ever learn? I cry for a few moments but know enough about my emotions to realise that they'll change.

The saviour of my depression comes in the form of a mop of blond hair rolling past on a skateboard.

'Hey Josh,' I shout, and run after him.

He kicks off his skateboard and turns to me. He has a surfboard under his arm and is still wearing the diamond earring. I explain my story and ask if I can transfer money into his account.

'No worries,' he says. 'I'm going for a surf first. I'll meet you in the competitors' area in two hours.'

Feeling reinvigorated I watch him leave. I form a new plan: I'll catch a train to Portugal for the next contest, get a replacement passport at the Australian embassy in Lisbon, go to the competition in Spain and then work in England for a month to save money for the rest of the surfing tour.

While waiting for Josh in the competitors' area, Nathan Hedge approaches me.

'I thought you were going to Paris?'

I try to explain about changing plans but he says 'Whatever' and brushes me off.

Half an hour later Matt Griggs walks up to me.

'What's going on mate?' he says.

'What do you mean?'

'We've heard all kinds of different stories about you. I thought you were going to Paris. What are you doing lurking around here asking people for money?'

'I'm not asking for money, I'm asking if I can transfer money into their bank account because my bank cards were stolen.'

'Is that right?'

Griggs, the Rip Curl team manager, is good-looking, tall, wears a fashionable Rip Curl jumper, and has stubble around his jaw.

'So you think I'm dodgy?' I reply defiantly. 'You're right, I'm actually an international money launderer.'

Griggs gives a look of bemusement, as if trying to work out whether I'm taking the piss.

'I'm not dodgy,' I add, then turn to face him. 'Besides, I don't have to justify myself to you anyway.'

At this point I don't care what professional surfers think of me—especially the Australians. We stare at each other for a few moments and then he walks off.

To clear my head, I surf on the peak next to the

competition and listen as the results drift over the ocean from the loudspeaker. Michael Campbell makes a tight heat and advances through to the next round. De Souza surfs beside me wearing a silver necklace. His surfing is lightning-quick and nimble and in comparison I feel like a sinking log.

'Are you still in the comp?' I ask, while we wait for the next wave.

'Yeah, I'm in a heat in an hour.'

I wish him luck and he thanks me and catches one in. I stay out for another hour. The waves are small but have a fair amount of power on the wedge. I hear de Souza win his heat convincingly and advance to the next round.

Back in the competitors' tent, I meet Josh and we go to an internet café and make the money transfer.

'It'll probably take a few days to come through,' he says. 'I'll let you know when it's in there.'

I thank him and walk through the town in the sunshine. Davi de Jesus and some of his Brazilian friends lay surfboards on a footpath, hoping to sell them to passers-by.

'How much are you selling this board for?' a French man asks Davi.

'200 euros,' he replies.

'I want to buy a board for my son. Is it possible to sell it cheaper?'

The man's request surprises me. The board looks new and is already a bargain.

'I'm sorry,' Davi replies, '200 is the price.'

The man disappears and comes back 30 minutes later with the money and the transaction is made. Davi, who has been knocked out of the contest before the money rounds, looks happy with the cash.

After spending an afternoon with the Brazilians I realise that life on the WQS is different for them than it is for the Aussies and Americans. It's about survival — if they don't make it as surfers, some have to go back to very poor families in Brazil. We laugh and joke and I try out my broken Portuguese, which I learnt three years ago from sharing a house with a bunch of crazy Brazilians in London.

I meet Victor Ribas. Victor is a regular campaigner on the WQS but has also made it onto the WCT. For years, I've seen photos of him in surfing magazines; he's probably been the most successful Brazilian in pro surfing. Yesterday in the contest area I'd overheard a story about him giving away a surfboard and wetsuit to a French kid who was learning.

Victor Ribas is short, friendly and has green eyes and a soft raspy voice. For a while he tells me about the surfers he knows from Margaret River.

'You must have had an amazing life as a professional surfer,' I say.

'Yeah, I've travelled a lot, met a lot of interesting people, broke up with my wife though.'

'Really, what happened?'

'I don't know, it just didn't work out, all the travelling I guess,' he says, raising his arms in contemplation.

Later, at an internet cafe, I catch a glimpse of Victor logged on to a dating website. I scour his profile and see his age: 32. This surprises me — after talking to him earlier, I know he is 34. The realisation that one of the most famous surfers in Brazil, and one of the nicest guys I've met, feels compelled to join a dating website and lie about his age hits me with sadness.

The following day I wake to the usual yelling from the commentator, who wants to clear the surf for the start of competition. I drag myself from the mattress, wander down to the sand, and then spend the day watching the contest. The semi-final between Jeremy Flores and Adriano de Souza is billed by the commentator as 'the future of professional surfing'. Admittedly, it is pretty good. Surfing 4-foot peaks, they go hell for leather, snapping through the sections and landing air reverses easily. With two minutes to go, Flores seals it with a 9. He's now due to face Michael Campbell in the final.

Mick has been fighting like an animal through heats all day. His surfing is beyond instinctive, like he somehow knows where the waves will break before they arrive. Even with this sixth sense, the younger surfers have a bag full of tricks and in most heats he's down until the final minutes before scraping through.

The crowd on the beach doubles in size for the final, eager to see Flores, the good-looking French teenager, win.

As Mick approaches the water inconspicuously, Flores is mobbed on the beach and spends ten minutes signing autographs. I realise that unless Flores falls off on every wave, the judges are going to let him win. But remarkably, Flores actually does fall twice in the final. On his first wave, he seems to lose his footing and slams his fist into the water in frustration. And then, with a minute to go and only needing a 6 to catch Mick, he digs a rail on a turn and is swallowed in the surf.

Onshore Mick is claimed by the other Aussie surfers. They thrust an Australian flag into his arms and carry him up the beach on their shoulders. I follow Mick into the competitors' area and congratulate him on the win.

'Thanks mate,' he replies, beaming.

A press conference is set up in the VIP area. Still in smelly shoes and looking dishevelled, I stand a few feet from Campbell and Flores and pretend to jot notes in a notepad to look authentic. The French press assemble around the room and spend 20 minutes asking Flores questions. When answering, Flores's eyes rarely raise from the floor. Most surfers would love to finish second in a 6-star event and have enough points to qualify for the WCT, but he clearly is not used to losing. The French journalists completely ignore Mick but this does not seem to bother him. He smiles across the room and gives the occasional thumbs-up to other surfers. After the press conference an awards ceremony is held on the main stage before about 500 people. The ceremony goes for an hour and is one of the silliest things I've ever seen.

The top three surfers stand on a dais, like the Olympics, and when Mick is announced the winner, gold confetti is sprayed into the crowd and the Australian national anthem is played. Mick, looking slightly embarrassed and no doubt feeling obliged to sing along, mumbles through the words.

Later, I sneak into a closing party held at a bar in town and indulge in free food and beer. The parties are keeping me fed. Somehow I've managed not only to survive for five days on €50, but also get drunk most nights.

At the after-party, I meet some French surfers and we walk to the nearby nightclub, then I blag us all in with a stolen competitor's pass. Pleased with my dodgy deeds, the French guys buy a round of drinks.

The nightclub is a haze of dancing girls, house music and tanned surfers. I spot two Hawaiian pro surfers in the centre of the dance floor. Feeling drunk, I approach them.

'Hey man, how's the party?' I ask one.

'Good,' he replies. 'We are the party.'

Thinking it's a joke, I laugh but he looks at me without expression and I realise he's serious. When they turn around I notice the back of their shirts have their names printed in bold lettering. I go back to the bar and wonder again why I'm on this silly tour, and how far outside the realm of reality you have to be to wear a shirt with your own name on it in a French nightclub.

Later, when I stumble back to the competitors' tent, a security guard is outside waiting for me.

'Sullivan, unfortunately there is a problem,' he states.

'What's wrong?'

'Your surfboards have been stolen.'

I go inside the tent to discover he's right—the board bag (which had contained all three boards and my wetsuit) is bare.

'Don't you guys patrol this area?' I ask.

'Yes, but we have a break between six and seven every night. The theft must have occurred then.'

I lie down on the empty board bag and cry.

'Would you like us to call the police?' he asks, seemingly unnerved by my tears.

'No, it's okay, don't worry, I'm always emotional when I drink.'

The security guard leaves and I curl up on the empty board bag and continue sobbing. Of course, it's not the theft of the surfboards as objects that upsets me. They're just foam and fibreglass and, apart from the 7' 10", which would have been handy in big waves, they've been the wrong choice. Yoman, from the surf shop in Indonesia, was right all along—the boards were too thin for me. Deep down, I know the real reason why I'm crying: The boards are linked to my identity as a surfer—something I never want to lose.

Re: entries
From: Brodie
Sent: Monday, 21 August 2006 8:55:38 AM
To: Sullivan McLeod

Hi Sully,

I can enter you in Portugal, however you will be on the alternate list for the trials. I will also keep your entry for the 4 star La Santa Pro.

Kind regards,

BJC
ASP Australasia Administration

Surfing Australia

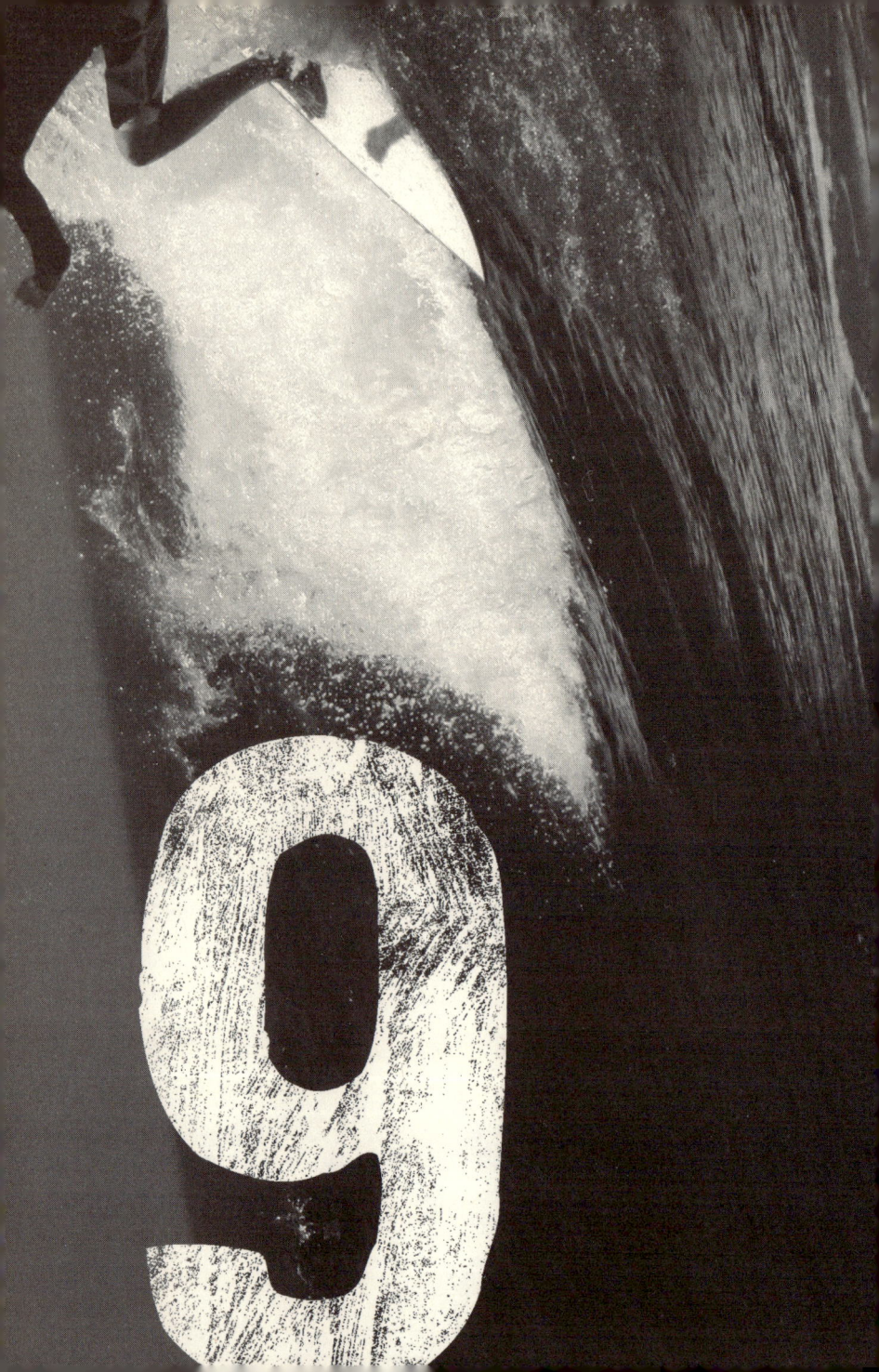

Portugal, August

In the morning after my surfboards are stolen, things appear brighter. I reassess the situation: There is another WQS competition that starts in two days at Hossegor, a beach an hour down the coast, but I may have left it too late to enter; besides, it feels like time to leave France. Meanwhile, one positive of the stolen boards is that I no longer have to lug them around the streets.

Deciding that it will look strange walking around with just an empty board bag, I leave it behind in the competitors' tent. I now have nothing but the smelly clothes on my back. Luckily, I bump into Josh Lewan on the street.

'Good news,' he says, thrusting €600 into my hand. 'The money you transferred into my account came through.'

To thank him, I buy lunch for us at a nearby café. As we eat he muses about all the strange intricacies of France — how it's hard to find a public toilet or butter for bread.

'For some reason I'm always really broke here,' he says, opening a croissant. 'Last year I couldn't find accommodation and ended up sleeping in a park. One night it poured with rain so I spent the entire night hiding in this little fort built for kids. The next morning I had to surf in my heat—I actually made it through.'

For an hour he keeps me entertained with stories about life on the WQS. When I ask him why he doesn't hang around the other Aussies on the tour, he replies: 'I spent my first six months with them but they never really accepted me. The way I look at it, I've gotta be true to myself.'

This statement takes me by surprise. Why does Josh Lewan, blond, young, good-looking, feel that he's not accepted by the core of his peers? After a few moments of contemplation I come to the conclusion that maybe the other pros don't relate to the diamond earrings and pop star aspirations. Not because they can't, but because they prefer not to. From what I've gathered, the young Aussie pros seem content chatting about last night's party, small complexities with their surfboards and what good-looking girls they've met on MySpace. Lewan's individuality is probably seen as a threat.

Josh Lewan has had an incredible life. At 22, he's ranked about 200th on the WQS, has had four round-the-world trips, gained and lost various sponsorships, been broke and homeless in at least five countries, and managed to seduce many young girls just for accommodation. Currently, he's staying with a young official of the contest—the same girl who'd contacted my dad.

In the afternoon he lends me a board and we surf the beach breaks. On a full tide with sloppy waves, Josh flies along the small wedges, easily combining airs and tail slides. Watching him from the water, I realise that I've not only underestimated him as a person but also as a surfer. Of course, I should have known that you don't make it into the top 200 on the WQS without having ability.

After the surf I say goodbye to Josh and leave Lacanau. At Bordeaux Central I buy a train ticket to Portugal for €120.

'You sure this will arrive in Lisbon?' I ask the girl at the ticket booth.

'Yes sir, I have even booked a sleeping carriage for you,' she replies with a smile.

I thank her, eat a cheese roll, and wait for the train to Portugal.

The journey from Bordeaux to Lisbon involves two trains. The first takes us to the border of Portugal. Here, there is a checkpoint where everyone must show their passports. In France I was warned by competition officials about travelling without a passport—most thought I was mad.

Luckily, the security at the checkpoint is lax; only two guards control a 200-metre line of people queued against a makeshift barrier. When the guards turn, I sneak under the barrier and board the train to Portugal.

In the dark corridor it takes a few minutes to find my cabin. My cabin is 3 metres wide and I share it with five others. There are three beds on either side that fold out like bunks. The passengers are four old people who look Portuguese and a blonde girl who is already asleep on the top bunk. I say hello to the passengers, find a bunk and fall asleep.

Throughout the night the train rattles and the other passengers exchange Portuguese conversation but I feel tired and drift in and out of sleep until sunrise. In the morning the cabin is empty apart from the blonde girl sleeping. I go to the bathroom to brush my teeth and when I return, the girl is sitting up on the bed.

'Where are we?' she asks, brushing the sleep from her eyes.

Her question takes me by surprise; there's a familiarity about it, as if we already know each other.

'I don't know, maybe an hour from Lisbon,' I reply.

I sit down on a seat in the cabin and the girl disappears to the bathroom. When she returns, she packs her bag and sits beside me. Her name is Louise. She looks about 25, is attractive, has an American accent and has been travelling around Europe for the past two months.

'So what are you doing over here?' she asks.

'Just travelling around,' I reply, realising that it'll be hard to pull off the 'professional surfer' card without actually having a surfboard.

I chat to Louise for 30 minutes. We're alone in the

cabin of a train traversing through Portugal. If I didn't lack confidence who knows what might have happened, but when the train stops we go our separate ways.

It takes me three hours to find a place to stay in Lisbon. After walking along old rocky roads and asking people for accommodation in broken Portuguese, I eventually find an internet café, order a coffee and analyse the sparse list of youth hostels. What follows is more broken Portuguese, tracking down two hostels that are full and eventually finding a room by accosting a stranger on the street. The room costs €10 a night. It's great to finally have a hot shower, and the water trickling down my back feels like it's cleansing away all the hassles of France. Feeling refreshed, I go to a nearby restaurant and eat a succulent meal of fish and salad.

The next day I go to the Australian embassy. I meet the senior consulate, a lady in her 50s. Without ID, applying for a passport should take days but I think she sees me as a long-lost son who has gone off the rails and a replacement is arranged within hours.

'It's only an emergency passport, which means it's only valid for seven months,' she says, handing it over. 'You'll need to change it when you get back to Australia.'

I thank her and leave. Although I still don't have bank cards, clothes, or even a surfboard, at least now I have a passport and a few hundred euros in my pocket. I feel like

I'm back in the game. Who knows, I might even make it to the other side of these haphazard penniless meanderings in one piece.

In the afternoon I catch a bus to Ericeira, the venue of the next surfing competition. Ericeira is a small town a few hours from Lisbon. When the bus stops at a desolate-looking petrol station, the passengers disembark.

'Is this Ericeira?' I ask the bus driver, a man with mousy black hair and a thick moustache.

'Yes.'

I survey the scene. There is nothing but limestone cliffs. I walk along the cliffs for about 500 metres and then arrive at a small cluster of shops. Two hundred metres further is a caravan park. Inside, I approach the lady behind the counter.

'Excuse me, do you know how much it is to stay here?'

'It depends. What kind of tent do you have?'

'I don't.'

'Pardon.'

'I don't have a tent.'

The lady is about 45, speaks clear English and glances at me with what seems to be empathy.

'Are you Australian?'

'Yeah. How did you know?'

'I recognise the accent. We have another Australian, Brett, who stays here. He's a nice guy. You should go and visit him and see if he's got a spare tent.'

I thank the lady, book into the caravan park for two nights and go searching for Brett. It doesn't take long to spot him. Brett is young, has stringy blond hair and can be distinguished as an Aussie from a mile off.

'Geez mate, you're travelling light,' he says, when I approach him.

I introduce myself and ask for a tent, feeling embarrassed and knowing that I'm assuming help on the fickle basis that we've both been born in the same country.

'No worries mate, I got bloody hundreds of 'em,' he replies.

I laugh.

'Nah seriously,' he adds. 'Every time someone takes off they leave a tent.'

He points to a cluster of tents beside us. 'They're all free.'

I thank him and he offers a beer. Having spent the past two weeks around professional surfers, I've forgotten about the warmth of normal Australians and we spend the night drinking and telling yarns around a fire.

The next morning four more Aussies arrive. They're Brett's friends from Cronulla and are also loud, tanned and jagged around the edges. Pretty soon it feels like we've created our own little Australian community. After Brett tapes together two wooden planks, we spend the morning playing cricket, smashing a tennis ball to all corners of the park. Occasionally the ball rolls into a stranger's tent and they throw it back with a smile.

At night we buy beer from a nearby store, swap travel stories around the campfire and then walk into the town to search for night-life. After drinking a few beers at a local bar, I make the mistake of telling the other Aussies about the surf tour.

'No shit,' says Warren, the square-shouldered mate of Brett. 'So you're one of those shit-hot surfers eh?'

'Nah, not really. Actually I had my boards stolen in France and was wondering if you guys were keen to sell me one.'

'Nah mate, I'm not a surfer,' he replies, sipping a beer thoughtfully, 'but you should ask Deano.'

Deano is tall, outgoing and blond and has been travelling through Europe for two months with Carpy, a kid with a mop of ragged hair. I can tell they are both surfers. When I ask them about boards, Deano replies: 'Yeah mate, we're off to the Greek islands next week. Not much surf to be had on the Mediterranean. I've got a nice little 6' 5" back at the campsite. I'll sell you the board for 100. Have you got a wet suit?'

'No.'

'You'll need one mate. Otherwise you'll be freezing your arse off in the water round here. I'll sell you my wetty for 50.'

I agree to the deal hastily and the next morning give Deano three €50 notes. There is now only €300 left from the €600 Josh had given me in France.

In the afternoon I search for surf with Deano and Carpy.

'There's a little right-hander that's not bad around here,' says Deano, but when we catch a glimpse of the ocean there are whitecaps on the horizon and the swells look messy.

'Bloody hell, too much wind,' he declares, and we head back to the campsite to start drinking.

Of course, with only €300 left and the contest starting in three days, I should stay off the booze but the quick banter, cheap wine and tinned spaghetti feels familiar and it's hard to say no to nostalgia.

The next day, after walking back from a surf-check, I spot Bobby Morris pulling out of the Ericeira caravan park in a hire car.

'Oi!' I shout, waving my arms.

He stops and winds down the window.

'Hey man,' he says, smiling, 'when did you get here?'

'Three days ago.'

He introduces me to Dasha, a girl beside him, who has flown over from the States to visit him.

'Where are ya staying?' he asks.

'In the caravan park.'

'No way,' he replies, thumping the dashboard with enthusiasm. 'So are we.'

'So where have you just come from?' I ask.

'The contest at Hossegor. It just finished.'

'How'd ya go?'

'Badly, I got knocked out in my first heat.'

'That sucks. Do you know who won?'

'Mick Campbell.'

'Nah, that's not right,' I tell him, 'Mick Campbell won Lacanau.'

'Yeah, I know, dumb ass,' he replies with a chortle, 'but he also won at Hossegor.'

They drive off to get supplies and back at the campsite I check the ASP website and discover Bobby is right. By winning at Hossegor, Mick has claimed two 6-star events in a row. Unbelievably, he's now leading the WQS.

The next morning I drive to the competition site with Bobby to check in. The venue for the contest is the main break at Ericeira—a long right which is apparently world class on its day but when we arrive the waves are 2 feet high and crumbly.

On the heat sheets I discover I'm up against a guy from Portugal, a Hawaiian, and a big-wave surfer called Peter Mel. I read over the name again. I've grown up watching videos of Peter Mel charging Waimea and Mavericks and wonder why on earth he's trawling through the beach breaks of Europe chasing WQS points.

At check-in, along with the usual stickers and magazines, I'm also given free food vouchers, which I'm happy about. I bump into Josh Lewan. He's wearing his trademark grin, unkempt hair and diamond earring.

'When did you arrive?' I ask.

'Last night—hell of a trip. Couldn't sleep on the train

and then I got down here at midnight with nothing booked. Had to crash out in my board bag on that footpath.'

He points to a wooden walkway which winds down the cliff to the beach. It doesn't look like a comfortable place to sleep.

'Was it cold?'

'Bloody freezing.'

'You should come up to the campsite and stay with us. It's only €4 a night.'

'Yeah, I might meet you there,' he says, and walks off to check into the contest.

Back at the campsite, the Aussies are roasting marshmallows and rattling off rude jokes. I buy a loaf of bread and ham and make sandwiches with Bobby and Dasha. We watch a Jean-Claude Van Damme movie on Bobby's laptop and then I go back to the tent and drop to sleep, listening to laughter escalate as the Aussies try to walk barefoot across the coals.

On the morning of the competition, I wake early and jog along the limestone cliffs with a stiff breeze on my back and the newly acquired €100 board tucked under my arm. At the beach, I realise I won't be favoured by the conditions—the waves are still small and lacking power. I stack my board, which has a crease on the nose and looks tanned beside the others, in a rack at the competitors' area and wonder if we're ever going to get decent waves on the European leg of the WQS.

At a booth near the competition site there's free internet

for competitors so I respond to some emails, hoping no one from home is watching the live webcast.

In the competitors' tent I meet Alex King, the Hawaiian in my heat. Alex is a polite, rosy-cheeked 17-year-old who I can already tell will be impossible to beat. He sits with another young Hawaiian, Mason Ho, who's the nephew of the famous Hawaiian surfer Derek Ho.

At the check-in area I'm given a blue vest. I change into it, wish Alex luck and we paddle out. As we wait for Peter Mel and the Portuguese surfer to join us, I realise that apart from drinking for three days and riding an unknown board in an unknown wetsuit at an unknown break, I've virtually left no stone unturned in my preparation.

Hoping to pick up any wide sets, I position myself to the side of the others. It's a bad strategy. Within two minutes a set of waves approaches and the other surfers pick them off, racking up scores between 5 and 7. As they paddle back, I see a lump of water moving on the outside; it's actually the best wave of the heat. I paddle hard and take off but the board feels strange under my feet and my movement is restricted by the wetsuit, which feels old and cumbersome. The wave has a nice shape and of course I should hit the lip but I play it safe and the manoeuvre comes off more like a soft floater. As the wave trails into the channel I manage a nice roundhouse cutback but fall at the finish.

As expected, the 17-year-old Alex is a flashy goofy-footer who rips. When I paddle back, he screams past me with three solid carves. The Portuguese commentator calls out the scores. I'm awarded a 4.5 for my first wave. Frankly, this surprises me. Maybe the judges have overestimated my ability; I only really completed a floater and then fell on a cutback.

I'm in fourth place but only need a mid-range score to move into second. As the others jostle for position on the peak, I catch a wide one but find it hard to gather speed and settle for a small re-entry on the inside. The wave scores a 2.5. The Portuguese surfer catches another nice ride and then Peter Mel picks one off and I'm left waiting out the back when the buzzer goes. I'm out in the first round again but for some reason it doesn't feel too bad.

'How'd ya go?' I ask Peter Mel as we're paddling in, feeling surreal to only be a foot away and staring into his eyes.

'Good,' he replies, 'I think I made it through.'

He seems in good spirits and his eyes are gentle but when my board bumps into his, he hardly breaks stride to push it away. It feels good to tease him.

In the afternoon I sit on the beach with Dasha and watch Bobby's heat. Although the waves are inconsistent and he struggles to find rhythm, he looks certain to advance until the final minute, when another surfer catches a wave and pushes him into third. He comes in looking shattered. For such a talented surfer, he's had a shocking European leg—only making it past the first round in one event.

'Where do you think I went wrong?' he asks, plonking down beside me on the sand.

'I don't know. Maybe you need to be a bit more patient and wait for the right waves.'

'Fuck,' he says, letting the sand run through his fingers, 'I've been competing for four years. This is the only thing I want to do and I still get knocked out in the first round.'

We remain silent.

'I'm going to cash in my lunch voucher,' I say eventually. 'Do you want anything?'

'Nah,' he replies, staring into the ocean.

At a caravan near the check-in area, I give a man my voucher and he returns with a packet of choc-chip biscuits, an apple and a drink that tastes like warm cordial. It's not exactly the best lunch but I'm thankful for anything. Moments later Josh cashes in his lunch voucher.

'How's it going?' I ask, as he rips open the packet of choc-chips and bites one.

'Pretty good.'

'Are you still sleeping on the footpath?'

'Nah, I got lucky.'

By chance, he'd met two local teenagers at the competition site yesterday who'd asked if he was in the contest. He told them he was and they offered him a place to stay.

'You should see this place. I think their oldies are pretty loaded. There's a pool and spa, they've been feeding me well and they even dropped me down here this morning.'

I bite my apple and laugh. It has taken him a day to go from sleeping on the footpath to a mansion.

I watch Josh's heat. Unfortunately, he suffers the same fate as Bobby and fails to catch the right waves, finishing third. Davi has an amazing heat. He looks gone but nails a wave in the final 20 seconds and scrapes through by a tenth of a point.

Back at the caravan park, the Aussies are already halfway through a carton of beer.

'How'd ya go mate?' Deano enquires.

'No good, got knocked out.'

'Bummer, how'd me board go?'

'Not bad, just need to get used to it.'

'Good shit,' he replies, and throws me a beer from the esky.

That night I go into town with the Aussies. I ask Bobby if he wants to join us but he's still down from his loss in the contest and declines. It's a beautiful town; there are narrow stone walkways and buildings that look old and peaceful. By contrast, every surfer who has been knocked out of the contest is being young and raucous. I spot Dean Randazzo, who's sitting at a table with a group of guys.

'Hey man, come over and have a beer with us,' he shouts.

I'd met Dean in Lacanau. He's an affable older-looking American. His pale skin and shaved head don't immediately earmark him as a pro but I'd seen him surfing in France and was surprised by his ability.

Dean's friends are all loud young pros who, in that typically American way, are blissfully unaware of the effect they're having on the local families sitting beside them. They're also quick to accept me as part of the group.

I sit with them for two hours, laughing at their antics. One of them looks like a young Patrick Swayze and converses in mad rhymes, occasionally approaching Portuguese girls and growling 'I'm a black cat prrrrrr'.

I find myself in a conversation with Dean. He talks about life growing up in New Jersey and his family. While he talks, I realise there's something strange about his face.

'Hey Dean,' I shout above the raucous mirth, 'why don't you have eyebrows?'

The table falls silent. For the first time in the night, the Americans look at each other self-consciously. Dean finishes the dregs of his beer and puts it down.

'I just finished chemotherapy.'

There is suddenly tension around the group.

'I'm sorry,' I say, staring down at the table.

'Don't worry about it,' he replies, looking at me with a wry grin. 'At least now I can tell girls I'm hairless all over.'

Everybody laughs. The tension eases. Another round of shots is ordered. Dean talks to me frankly about his cancer. He's been fighting it for the past year and has only finished the treatment last month.

'You're in this comp only a month after chemo?' I ask, stunned.

'Yep, but I got knocked out in the first round—I'm only just getting my strength back. Reckon I'll give it another few weeks before I feel confident that I can start getting through heats.'

I sit back and realise that I'm now peering across the landscape of the tour from a different perspective. Forget the gung-ho Brazilians, who travel the world on a shoe-string, forget Josh Lewan, who trades in charm, forget Mick Campbell, who hit the tour like a shot from the blue, the real story of the WQS is Dean Randazzo.

Later, one of the Americans turns to Dean and says: 'Hey man, when did you qualify for the WCT?'

'Back in 1996,' he replies.

'You've been on the WCT?' I ask. I was immersed in surfing back then and wonder why I haven't heard of him.

'Yeah.'

'You know, you've still got one of the best forehand carves I've ever seen bro,' another chimes in, and slaps Dean on the back.

'When I was a kid I had a poster of you up on my wall,' says the surfer on the other side of the table. 'You were on this right going straight up at the lip with your hand on the rail. I tried for years to do a move like that. I'd go out in crappy little beach breaks and have my hand on the rail just like yours, but I could never do it.'

There's a message behind the compliments. They respect him. They want him to know that he's an inspiration. They see him as a fighter. For a brief moment emotion sweeps over Dean's face, then he snaps out of it.

'What is this? Ya trying to make me puke? Shut up and drink.'

The Americans laugh and chink his glass and I know that it won't matter if I go to Hawaii and catch the wave of my life at Pipe, it won't matter if I somehow sneak the bomb set off the pack at Waimea, it won't even matter if, for some miraculous reason, I start making heats. I realise, in that brief moment when Dean's face clouded with emotion, that I've just witnessed the best thing that will happen on this tour.

Re: competitions
From: Brodie

To: Sullivan McLeod

Hi Sully,

I have entered you in the following competitions:
* 3 STAR FERROLTERRA PANTIN CLASSIC – SPAIN
* 5 STAR BUONDI BILLABONG PRO – PORTUGAL
* 2 STAR 9TH O'NEILL TROPHY – CANARIES
* 3 STAR LA CAJA DE CANARIES – OCEAN AND EARTH PRO
– CANARIES
* 4 STAR LA SANTA PRO – CANARIES

How would you like to pay for these? I can't enter you in the competitions without a payment method. Your confirmation number for these entries is 669.

Cheers,

James
In office for Brodie until 27th of July
ASP Australasia Administration
Surfing Australia

Spain, September

And so the locomotive that is the WQS packs up and goes storming off down the track to the next venue. Contest vests are numbered and stored. Electronic judging devices are carefully placed inside boxes. The hooter to signal the end of each heat is tested and packed away. The judges themselves will check out of their hotel, consume their continental breakfast and orange juice, chat with each other about who should have really won the last event, and speculate on who will win the next.

At the next venue, posters will be displayed in shop windows. A teenager will see the posters and tell his parents every night that the surfers are coming, the surfers are coming, and not sleep for three days.

Somewhere, above some beach, temporary seating will be temporarily erected. Men will sweat over shovels, bolting together steel iron girders and hammering wooden planks. They will not be getting paid much, but will laugh and joke and play practical jokes on each other. There will be girls who will agree to work on the contest site for no money, but the pay-off of idle banter with the pros will be hard to come by because the pros are not good with idle banter, and most will fail to realise that this is why these girls have volunteered their time.

Surf companies at board-room level will employ reps, and the reps will emerge at the contest sites scouring for the next bright-eyed surf star. They will not necessarily sponsor the most talented or best young surfer, but the one who they think will appeal to what their market requires. And if the future stars are sponsored they'll be given free boards and wetsuits and appear on magazine pages but most will never make it onto the WCT.

And those on the fringes of the WQS will shove their boards into a board bag, check the ASP website to see if they've advanced up the ratings and somehow make their way, by bus or plane or train or hire car, to the next contest.

And at the end of each year fifteen dreams will be made, and hundreds of others will not be shattered, but momentarily put on hold until next year, when the registration fees are paid, the plane tickets are purchased, the quiver of boards are tightly packed and the journey can begin again.

*

I'm on the road with Bobby and Dasha. They've offered me not only a lift in their hire car to the next contest in Spain, but also a sleeping bag and some clothes, which I'm grateful for. With the competition a few days off, we're in no rush to arrive in Spain and so we check out surf spots along the way.

At one of these breaks, a weak but long right straight out in front of a beachside café, we surf by ourselves for two hours and then we're joined by another surfer. The man, who looks like a friendly local in his thirties, paddles beside me and sits up on his board.

'Hello,' he says.

'Oi com esta?' (How are you?) I reply, eager to try out my Portuguese.

'Bane.'

After waiting a few moments for the next wave, he turns to me.

'Were you a competitor at the WQS competition in Ericeira?'

'Yes,' I reply, flabbergasted.

He has assumed I'm a pro surfer—something that has never happened in my entire life. Of course, it may be the timing—that we're white guys surfing in a remote break straight after the competition has finished—or that I'm surfing with Bobby, who is ripping. But either way, he still assumed I was a pro.

When growing up I was told a story about a poor peasant

in ancient Egypt who, to join the king's circle, disguised himself in the mask of a rich knight. One day, after the peasant had worn the mask for years, the king became curious and asked him to remove it. Underneath was a rich knight—the peasant had been wearing the mask so long his face had moulded into it. Maybe I'm the peasant who has been wearing the pro surfer mask so long my face has moulded to it.

The local surfer is quickly hospitable and shows us a secret surf spot in the afternoon. The secret spot is on the other side of an old lighthouse. It's a fun right which we surf with a handful of others for a few days, then we say goodbye and drive across the border into Spain.

We arrive at Pantin, the town that will host the next contest, on a foggy evening as the last of the sun's light disappears under the horizon. I jump out of the hire car excitedly, rush down to the beach and peer out through the mist.

'How big is it?' Bobby shouts from the car.

'I don't know, there's too much fog to tell.'

After we book into a dodgy-looking caravan park, I curl up inside the borrowed sleeping bag and fall asleep.

In the morning we eat cereal and then drive down to the contest site to discover the fog still hanging stubbornly over the ocean. The consensus is made by officials to wait until the fog clears before they start the contest. They need not have bothered. When it clears, the ocean looks like a lake—there's not a single wave breaking.

'Attention surfers,' I hear from the speakers, 'we have decided to delay the competition until tomorrow, there appears to be a new swell on the way. Please check back here at 8.30 tomorrow morning.'

I go back to the campsite with Bobby and Dasha. We eat ham and cheese sandwiches and then drive into town. At an internet café, I check the results of the Ericeira comp and discover the winner was a local Portuguese surfer called Tiago Pires. Davi had been knocked out before the money rounds. Mick Campbell, who was also knocked out early, has now relinquished his lead on the WQS to Jeremy Flores.

The next morning at the beach we're greeted with the good news of the fog clearing and the swell picking up—instead of being dead flat, the waves are now waist high. The officials decide to start the competition. At check-in, I discover that I'm an alternate surfer; I have to wait until someone pulls out before they'll let me compete.

'What should I do now?' I ask Gregoire, the ASP rep, who seems to eye me warily these days.

'Just wait around on the beach,' he says. 'I'll let you know if you're in.'

I chat with Josh. He does most of the talking but I don't mind. Listening to his low-pitched drawl feels soothing, like drinking a cup of hot chocolate in winter. He tells me another entertaining story. After discovering the competition had been delayed yesterday, he'd walked to a bus stop to catch a bus into town. While waiting, a local girl had sparked a conversation with him from a nearby house. She invited him inside. Thinking that the prospect of a bus was slim anyway, he accepted. Once inside, however, he realised the house did not belong to the girl but her parents, an old couple who couldn't speak a word of English. Needless to say, they were a tad concerned that their daughter had invited an unknown gringo into the house. For the next three hours, the daughter translated everything he said and invited him to stay for dinner. Later, they made up a bed for him in the spare room and, in the middle of the night, the girl snuck out of her room and crawled into his bed.

'Yep,' he says, smiling as he peers across the waves breaking on the beach, 'this is a beautiful country.'

I laugh and realise that someone should follow him for a year with a video camera and turn his life into a movie.

Bobby Morris rushes up to me.

'Hey man, they've been calling out your name over the speakers.'

'Really?'

'Yeah, hurry, you might be in the next heat.'

I rush over to the check-in area. A South African surfer has pulled out of the contest and I have the option to replace him. I agree to surf in the heat and Bobby runs up the beach with my board. By the time I reach the sand, the hooter goes off. There are two rideable peaks. While the three other competitors sit on a sandbank to the right, there are also ten recreational surfers on a sandbank to the left that is within the competition zone.

'Where do you think I should surf?' I ask Bobby, as I throw the vest over my head.

'Sit with the other guys,' he replies, pointing to the three competitors.

'But I'll have any wave I want on the other peak.'

'Yeah, but it's not breaking there.'

He wishes me luck and I jump into the ocean and paddle for the peak being surfed by people not in the competition.

'Excuse me recreation surfers, can you please clear the line-up for the competition,' I hear; it's then repeated in Spanish. I watch the recreational surfers scatter and feel powerful, like I'm parting the red sea. At the sandbank I sit on my board and wait and wait and wait. Of course, Bobby is right. The waves approach, threaten to break and then peter out. After ten minutes I've only managed to stand once for five seconds. The 1.2 I'm awarded is another overscore.

After a few more minutes waiting I swallow my pride and paddle frantically to the other peak. By the time I reach the other competitors, there's only ten minutes left. I sit beside them and smile. One, the guy in the blue vest, smiles back. When a small set of waves approaches we scramble for position. The guy in the red vest, who looks Australian, catches the first wave of the set and rides it well. The second wave breaks too far out and the third wave is mushy and I share it with the guy in the white vest—he goes right and I go left. The wave is small and I surf it badly, somehow not finding enough speed to make it around the whitewater. I'm awarded 1.5.

The hooter sounds moments later and I go in feeling embarrassed.

Bobby approaches me on the beach.

'I told you to go to the other peak,' he says, shaking his head, but his voice is soft and sympathetic.

'I'm giving up these stupid competitions,' I sulk, peeling my wetsuit from my arms.

'Hey, it's not that bad, you actually beat someone,' he laughs.

In the competitors' area I learn that the surfer in the blue vest had only caught one wave—a 2.2. My combined total of 2.7 had trumped him. I'm awarded 128 points for placing third. Remarkably, it will probably move me another 50 places up the ratings. I have another epiphany—perhaps it's worth giving up drinking and taking these competitions seriously after all.

The next day Bobby surfs for the first time on a rising swell. He dominates his heat, scoring an 8.5 and a 9. With a minute to go he catches a fast right, hits the lip and gracefully lands an air 360 which sparks loud whistling from the crowd. Later, I see a photo of the air on the ASP website—it's described as the best manoeuvre of the contest.

After Bobby's heat we go to a café beside the competition venue and eat lunch with Josh. Having run out of money, I ask Josh if I can transfer another €300 into his account and he agrees.

In the afternoon, after going into town to put money into Josh's account, I meet Liam McNamara. McNamara is a famous Hawaiian who's well known for charging massive tubes at Pipe. I've grown up seeing him surf in videos and magazines and it feels surreal to stand on a beach in Spain and be in an amicable conversation with him. During the event I've watched him giving advice to young Hawaiians and, although he's in the event, I suspect his involvement is more about being a mentor than a competitor.

As the week progresses, Bobby looks certain to win the competition. He dominates everything until the quarter-finals. In the quarters he takes a patient approach, passing up many waves until, with five minutes to go, he gets a long right and scores 6.5. With three minutes left he only needs 4 to advance. I'm watching the contest with Dasha on a hill overlooking the beach.

'Do you think he's going to make it?' she asks me.

'Yeah he'll be right, only needs a 4,' I reply, but with a minute to go I know the odds are remote.

Then, in the final 30 seconds, he picks off an insider and fits in a few good snaps.

'Should be enough,' I say.

The score comes through as we walk down to the

beach. It's a 3.5. Bobby has finished third. He comes in dejected and stays in a bad mood for an hour.

'You know, I can't work out these competitions,' he says later. 'Where do you think I went wrong?'

'I don't know,' I reply.

I have no answers. How someone like Bobby Morris—who is intensely focused, lightning quick and has a combination of old-school carves and new-school airs to impress the judges—can't make it into the top 100 let alone the top 15 on the WQS perfectly illustrates how hard the tour is.

'We're gonna drive back to France, do you want a lift?' he asks.

'Nah, my flight leaves from Lisbon. Besides, I've gotta wait for Josh till my money comes through.'

'Hang on a sec,' he says, and reaches into the hire car. 'This is from Josh.'

He hands me €300.

'Did the money come through?'

'Nah but he had to leave after being knocked out of the comp this morning and trusts ya.'

I accept the money, feeling like a goose and realising how much I'd initially misjudged Josh. He not only helped in France but has now given me money even though it is yet to show up in his account.

I say goodbye to Bobby and Dasha and, as their car is just out of shouting range, I suddenly realise I've left my emergency passport on their back seat. Feeling like a fool, I chase them but it's too late. I watch their hire car slowly wind through the hills of Pantin. Cursing, I pick up a rock and hurl it at a nearby bin and hear the 'ping' as it rebounds away. They have no contact number. The only thing I can do now is send an email to them and hope they get it before they fly back to America.

On the way back to the contest site I bump into Liam McNamara.

'Hey buddy, could you do me a favour?'

'What's that?' I ask, realising that it'd take an enormous amount of willpower to turn down a guy like Liam.

'Well, we're catching a flight back to Hawaii. I was wondering if you could make a speech for Tonino Benson. He won an award for the best surfer under 21 in the competition but won't be around to collect it. Just say a few words thanking the organisers and the town of Pantin.'

'No worries, I can do that,' I reply, immediately feeling a strange rush of pride and dread. Why has Liam picked me to make the speech? And what if I stuff it up?

'Thanks bro,' he says and slaps me on the back. 'I'll see you in Hawaii.'

Davi de Jesus hits form in Pantin, easily making it into the quarters. In his quarter-final, because of a technical problem in the commentary area, all sound is lost so it's hard to know who's winning. Davi catches two good waves but so do the others. When the quarter-final ends, I spot him in the car park.

'How'd ya go Davi?'

He gives me a broad smile and two thumbs-up.

Eager for a good vantage point for the semi-finals, I find a spot on the beach directly in front of the waves. In the first semi-final, Davi is up against two Americans, Patrick Gudauskus and Austin Ware, and a fellow Brazilian, Tanio Barreto. The waves are now the biggest they've been for the entire event but are also inconsistent and it's quickly apparent that the surfers must make the best of anything that comes through. Halfway through the heat, I watch a nice wave forming, easily the best so far. Barreto, who sits closest to the breaking wave, attempts to take off but pulls back at the last minute. Davi, who's in the perfect position, also pulls back and Gudauskus swings late and milks it through to the inside. When the hooter sounds Davi is in third and the two Americans advance through to the final.

I watch Davi making his way past spectators up the beach.

'Unlucky bro,' I say, in an attempt to console him.

'Did you see that?'

'See what?'

'Tanio, he spooked me on the best wave of the day.'

'What happened?'

'It doesn't matter,' he says, placing his surfboard into the hire car with care. The board is plain apart from a small sticker of a lizard on the nose. It looks too small for Davi's square shoulders but I know it's his favourite — his only board left. He'd sold the others in Lacanau to have enough money to travel to the rest of the European competitions. Being a professional surfer with only one board is a calculated risk but I know, as I watch him peel the contest vest from his shoulders, that his life is as much about risks as it is surfing. With the €1500 he's won in this event, he now has enough money to make it to the Canary Islands for the next competition.

'We're driving back to Ericeira, do you want a lift?' he asks me.

'That would be great but I have to make a speech for someone. Do you mind waiting until after the presentations?'

'Sorry man, we have to leave now. Don't worry about the speech, it's not your responsibility.'

I consider it. Liam McNamara, having gone back to Hawaii, will not know if I make the speech. Besides, I'll feel like an idiot on stage.

Davi collects his prize money and I jump into the hire car beside two other Brazilian pros and a surfer from Portugal. We leave before the start of the final but their haste hardly surprises me. Their decisions are based on emotion—it's in the South American blood.

In a town along the way, we stop at a Portuguese restaurant and they laugh when tricking me into eating a traditional dish, which is a kind of raw curry swamped in blood. Then we jump back into the car and Davi drives like a maniac through the night while they laugh and joke and shout in Portuguese. I feel tired and, unable to keep my eyelids open, drift to sleep sensing that we're about to crash at any moment.

London, September

From afar, Heathrow in late September looks the same as usual. The ground crew wear bright yellow tops and actively flock around the tarmac. Customs officers are cold and bristly. At check-in, girls behind the counters are usually young, a tad overweight and have northern English accents. In the interests of airport safety, things that do not need to be reported are reported—over a loudspeaker.

I'm sitting in an airport café, sipping a coffee and waiting for my flight to the Canary Islands. With an hour to kill, I glance around and wonder why the café is deserted. After a few minutes of serious thinking I resolve that the simple reason—that buying one single coffee in Heathrow costs roughly the same as buying a whole herd of camels in Egypt—is not the answer. Having lived in England, I know middle-class Londoners like nothing more than having the appearance of people who can, if they choose to, squander money.

At Heathrow, coffee is sold for double the price of a standard cup in London (which is already double the price of the rest of Europe). I don't consider a muffin but one day I might, purely for shock value. By rights, even if the price of a coffee at Heathrow is the equivalent of a taxi fare in Norway, the middle classes should be indulging. But they don't. And the reason I've come up with—the stubborn bastards refuse to believe it's cold enough. As the September temperatures plummet, they cling to the concept of summer. You have to admire their steely resolve—they're still wearing pleated skirts, short-sleeve shirts and erect nipples.

Alright, I'm being harsh on London and Londoners. It really is an amazing place to an amazing lot of people and I must admit I've just had the time of my life here.

To tie up a few loose ends: Josh has flown back to Australia to meet with the Universal record label. Bobby is back in America; hopefully I'll catch up with him in Hawaii. Davi de Jesus did actually crash the hire car in Portugal. Being asleep at the time I have no idea how. Fortunately he crashed the car into (and I swear I'm not making this up) a friendly panelbeater who was happy to fix all damage free of charge. The crazy cat is now on the Canary Islands. I plan to see him at the next surf contest on the island of Lanzarote in a few days.

I managed to get my passport back in Portugal and a replacement bank card in London. The passport drama was not easy. While continually jamming coins into a hungry payphone outside the Ericeira caravan park, I tracked it down to a hotel in Paris where Bobby had left it and somehow managed to convince a camp porter who spoke little English to send it back. Miraculously, the passport showed up a few days later and I boarded my flight to England.

In London, things didn't start well. I arrived to discover my surfboard in two pieces. In the airline's defence, the sticky tape and foam I'd used as a makeshift board bag was not exactly sturdy. My plan of making money fast also stumbled when I discovered I was homeless. My brother had a Polish girlfriend living with him and refused to let me doss in his room. Possibly feeling a little guilty, my brother lent me his spare clothes and then spent a few days calling people, most of whom he barely knew, and eventually, after I agreed to pay £45 a week, he found someone willing to harbour me.

The guy I stayed with was a magician who turned out to be one of the most incredible characters I've ever met. The Magician was a young South African who earned money by performing street magic in London. He shared a tiny two-bedroom council flat with a 45-year-old Scotsman who I never saw in anything other than a dressing-gown. The Magician had the smaller of the two rooms. Later, in a curious mood, I actually measured it. (Four paces long and two wide.) When I first entered the room, I wondered where we were going to sleep—the floor was crammed with magic props and the walls were filled with handwritten notes like 'I will have 4 325 567 pounds and 24 pence by February 8th 2009'.

'What are these?' I asked, pointing at the notes.

'Affirmations,' he replied cheerfully.

Unfortunately, he also had verbal affirmations. Although listening all night to a loud tape saying 'You will own a luxury unit above the Thames' was uplifting, sleep was hard to come by.

One day, I asked the Magician about his magic and soon found myself being part of his show. We arranged it so I would walk past during his act and he'd invite me over. With the audience unaware that we actually knew each other, we bounced off each other with some funny lines and it worked pretty well. Through being a stooge in the Magician's show, I met some of his friends. One of these, a computer hacker, is in fact the most incredible person I've met in my life. Right now, as I'm about to board my flight, I still don't know how much to believe.

Here's what I do know: Hacker performed street magic in London. Hacker was 32 years old, Jewish, wore a ponytail and black jacket, had intense shining eyes and, up until a year ago, was one of the most famous and brilliant computer hackers in the world. Hacker seemed affronted by the word magician and called himself a mentalist. Hacker demonstrated to me the most mind-blowing things I'd ever seen and, the truth is, I'm still not sure they were even tricks. He correctly predicted what I was thinking before I said it. He could immediately calculate the cubed root of a number in the millions (he proved this one night and I checked it with a calculator). He remembered a list I invented of 50 bizarre things (like the hair of a pig's hindquarter) and then repeated them to me without making a single mistake four days later.

Hacker owes roughly 6 million pounds to the British government. After entering a plea bargain to get out of jail, he was attempting to pay it back by working at Scotland Yard between the hours of midnight and 8 a.m. probably to sort out very important secret computer codes and passwords.

This is what I'm unsure about: Hacker claimed he could see energy. Although sceptical, I had an open mind about the idea and he taught me a technique, staring at a gap between your fingers every morning for 30 minutes, which apparently develops this ability. (I tried this for a few days but gave up after nothing much happened.)

Hacker claimed that sleeping under an old tree will give you energy. Hacker claimed to have spent a whole week holding up a sign in the centre of London with the word 'smile' on it, because he was worried about people's misguided priorities. Hacker claimed to be able to speak 12 languages fluently. Hacker claimed to be owed free accommodation at some 5-star hotels in the Middle East after helping out a sultan's nephew by hacking into a computer system and updating a driver's licence. Hacker claimed he was one of only three people in the world who could card count (where you remember the cards in a deck) up to eight decks, and, because of that, he was not allowed to play at most of the casinos in the world. (I saw him card count one pack but not eight, and we never went to a casino.)

After a few days in London I was employed by a friend of my brother to sell sepia photographs at an inner-city market stall. This was all good with one exception—I knew nothing about sepia photography. As usual I blagged it and pretended I knew what I was talking about. This technique was fairly fruitful until a well-educated lady who, it turned out, knew a heck of a lot about sepia photography asked me a few questions.

Later, I discovered that the knowledge of the photographs was not important. The Londoners were content with a smiling face and a few jokes and I left the job with a few pounds saved.

So that was my three weeks—goal-oriented magicians, strange geniuses and highbrow photography. Who says London is boring? Plus, I also failed to seduce an Australian girl on a Contiki tour and a Brazilian waitress.

Canary Islands, October

Soon after disembarking my plane in Lanzarote, an island in the Canary Islands, I realise that I've lost my plane tickets to Brazil and Hawaii. In a panic, I ask the airline for help, hoping they can duplicate the tickets. After ten minutes of going through the specifics of flight directions and routes at a customer service counter, I feel a lump in my back pocket. The tickets, as it happens, are not lost in transit. Coincidently the stuff-up is fortuitous because I discover that my flight to Brazil is due to leave in two days.

'This can't be right,' I declare, handing the newfound tickets to the friendly girl at customer service who no doubt wishes she'd never laid eyes on me.

'Yes sir, this is what the ticket says,' she confirms. 'Your flight to Brazil leaves in two days.'

'But I'm meant to be here for a week to compete in a surfing contest in Lanzarote. Any chance you can change it?' I ask, eager to see how far the 'professional surfer' card will ride.

She sighs and bangs away on the keyboard.

'I'm sorry. I can't.'

'What do you mean you can't?'

'I mean it's not possible for me to change your flight to Brazil.'

'Why not?'

'Because the airline you're with has recently gone broke and now only does one flight a week into Brazil, which means all flights there are booked for the next three months. Alternatively, you can purchase another ticket with a different airline.'

'How much will that cost?'

'Depends on the airline, but most last-minute flights from here to São Paulo would probably be in excess of €1000.'

'A thousand euro, I can't afford that.'

'Well sir, it looks as if you have no choice but to catch your flight in two days.'

And so, with the prospect of competing in Lanzarote now dashed, I stay in a hostel for two days watching badly dubbed Hollywood movies (I don't know Spanish but come to the conclusion that it doesn't matter with Hollywood movies) and then catch my flight to São Paulo.

RE: Onbongo Pro Event Information
From: Brodie
Sent: Tuesday, 26 September 2006 7:33:54 AM
To: Sullivan McLeod

Hi Sully,

I have recorded your entry into the 6 star Onbongo Pro. Your entry confirmation number is 797.

You can send me your credit card details and we can process the payment that way or you can send a cheque or a money order. The entry fee is $310 AUD. I will include you on the entry list as today is the entry deadline. If you however decide to withdraw please let me know within the next 4 days so I can withdraw you without penalty. (If you withdraw later than 1 October you will still be required to pay for the entry fee.)

Kind regards,

BJC
ASP Australasia Administration
Surfing Australia

Brazil, November

Apart from five years ago, when I conned a German girl into driving with me across the San Diego border into Mexico and then promptly got us lost for 12 hours (sparking a dislike towards me so severe that she still refuses to answer my emails), I've never been to Central or South America and feel excited walking through the airport in São Paulo. At customs, the excitement is quickly replaced by fear.

The customs officer, a young man with broad shoulders and dark eyes, spends five minutes flicking through my passport with a quizzical expression.

'Where is your visa?' he says finally, his eyes resting on mine.

'Visa, what visa?'

'The visa you need to enter this country.'

Reality hits. I purchased my visa for Brazil in Australia — it has been stolen with my original passport.

'This is only an emergency passport,' I explain. 'My real passport with my visa was stolen in France.'

'Sir, can you please step to the side?' he says; it's more a statement than a question.

He directs me to a bench beside the customs booth. I wait for 20 minutes and watch as streams of people have their passport stamped and slip through to the airport foyer. Two Chinese guys wearing ragged jeans and torn denim jackets sit beside me.

'What are you guys in for?' I ask, but they don't speak English and remain silent.

'Excuse me Sullivan,' I hear, and turn to see an airport official walking briskly towards me. 'Can you please follow me?'

I follow the man through a series of corridors that lead into a room full of people.

'Sit here,' he says, pointing at a bench.

I sit on the bench and stare up at a sign that says 'Departure Lounge'.

The man returns moments later.

'You have no visa to be in this country. You are going to be deported back to Europe. The plane leaves in 20 minutes.'

'I don't think so,' I reply, surprising myself with a calm voice.

'No?'

'No, I'm not going anywhere,' I repeat, feeling tired and detached.

'Well sir, then I'm afraid we will have to get the police to escort you,' the customs officer says; they will be his last words in English.

He retrieves a walkie-talkie from his pocket and speaks rushed Portuguese into it. Moments later, two policemen arrive.

'Hello sir,' one says cordially. 'Unfortunately you don't have a visa for this country and we have to escort you onto a plane going back to the Canary Islands.'

They grab me by the arms and lead me towards the departure gate.

'Oi, let go of me.'

Their reply is forceful and in Portuguese. I think back to living with Brazilians. My mind scrambles for Portuguese words. Suddenly, the words appear in my mind. I break from their grip and shout: 'Eu vou irr pada nada agora.' (I'm not going anywhere now.)

They stare at me in bewilderment.

'Look guys, I know you're just doing your job,' I continue in English, 'but I'm too tired to get on a plane for 14 hours, and I'm not going anywhere until I speak to the Australian embassy.'

'You have no choice,' one of the policemen replies.

'You can try all you want but I'm not getting on that plane,' I reiterate.

'Well sir, then we have to take you to a holding cell, and there are no guarantees for how long you will be there.'

'Fine, take me to the holding cell,' I say, thinking they're bluffing.

Five minutes later I'm in the holding cell—it turns out they're not.

The holding cell is not as bad as it sounds. It's a room on the second floor of the airport that's actually twice the size of the Magician's room in London. Inside, there are two chairs and a couch. The door is always open but any escape attempt will be foolish. Not only is my backpack (a second-hand one I bought in London) under lock and key but I'll have to negotiate past a guard.

I plonk myself down on the couch. I need to think, to find a way out. My brain feels tired and reluctant to tackle the task. I approach the guard.

'Oi, eu quira Autralie embassy.' (I want the Australian embassy.)

The guard rattles off Portuguese too fast to understand.

'Do you know if I can call the Australian embassy?' I ask.

He stares at me blankly. Communication will not be easy. The guard wears a crisp white shirt, has a friendly face and is young—I guess about five years younger than me. His demeanour is not rude and the silence seems more from not knowing English than a desire to ignore me. Reasoning that the guard's English is worse than my Portuguese I realise, with dread, that all conversation from now on must be in Portuguese. I have a genius idea (that I'll consider ridiculous later) to teach the guard English. When his knowledge is sufficient to understand my problems, I'll simply negotiate my way out.

I spend three hours teaching the guard English. Strangely, he doesn't seem to find the process patronising and is an avid learner. With a pen and paper, he copies what I write in Portuguese and I tell him the translated meaning in English. Just as I'm about to have a breakthrough, the young guard is replaced by an old man with a stern expression.

I go back to the couch. Throughout the night sleep is difficult because my legs do not fit the couch and I'm constantly harassed by mosquitoes.

In the morning I check outside the holding cell to discover the sober-faced old guard staring back at me. It's day two. I need a plan. The guard comes into the room and speaks rushed Portuguese. He wants me to follow him. He leads me through the airport and into a café, and then he orders a coffee and turns to me: 'Eat, you want?'

He hands me a voucher. I'm allowed to spend €10 at the café. I buy a ham and salad roll, a coffee and a brownie and we eat the food in silence.

When we return I discover a new person in the holding cell. The man, who is well-dressed and looks about 60, does not fit the mould of a hardened criminal. He says hello and introduces himself as Peter. He's a German conductor of an orchestra touring through South America. After his luggage had been lost, he'd called a girl at the customer service area a bitch and now they want to deport him back to Germany.

'If it wasn't true it would be laughable,' he says, shaking his head with disbelief.

'Ya gotta watch out for these South Americans,' I reply. 'They have a lot of passion.'

We spend an hour chatting. Peter is well-spoken and funny and I appreciate the company.

He pulls a mobile phone from his pocket and makes a call in German. 'That was the German embassy,' he tells me, when finished.

'Can they help you?'

'Maybe. You should call the Australian embassy.'

'I don't have their phone number.'

'Hang on a second,' he says.

He makes a call, surprising me by speaking fluent Portuguese. During the call he takes a notepad from his pocket and begins jotting down something.

'This is the number of the Australian embassy in São Paulo,' he says, and hands over the piece of paper and his mobile phone.

I thank him and call the Australian embassy. A lady answers immediately. It has never felt so good to hear an Australian accent. I tell her my situation.

'I'll look into it,' she responds calmly. 'I'll call you back in 20 minutes.'

Twenty minutes later the mobile rings.

'I've been in contact with the chief of police at the airport,' she tells me. 'We can get you out.'

'Really?'

'Yes but I'm more worried about your next stop, which is Hawaii. Your emergency visa is only valid for another five months and the Americans require six. You have to come into the Australian embassy in São Paulo and apply for another passport.'

'Okay, I'll do that. Thanks for your help.'

An hour later a plain-clothed official, I guess a policeman, approaches the holding cell and exchanges Portuguese with the guard.

'You got a break surfer boy,' the policeman says, and hands over my backpack. 'We're giving you a visa for eight days, so you can compete in your surfing competition. It would be wise not to overstay it.'

I say goodbye to Peter and wish him luck, then the policeman leads me through a series of checkpoints. I sign some paperwork, put my backpack through an X-ray machine and then walk through to the airport foyer. Outside, I hardly notice the rain. I haven't slept for two days but don't feel tired. I've barely eaten but don't feel hungry. I'm happy. I catch a bus into the city, eat a sandwich, find a cheap hotel and have a blissful sleep.

I wake early the next morning and, of course, get lost trying to find the Australian embassy. Finally, I catch the right train and I travel past half-built homes and clothes hanging on rusty clotheslines. It's clear the Brazilians are a resilient lot. Even in areas of extreme poverty, the children smile and happily play hopscotch.

Two incidents happen on the train that illustrate the Brazilian character. On board, it's so packed that two girls squash up beside me. The girls, who look about 20, are not self-conscious with my presence and chat with each other openly. They have clear brown skin, green eyes and look stunning. I don't understand their conversation but their expressions are vast and they laugh freely. Only inches from their faces, I watch in wonder, amazed at how uninhibited they are. When my stop arrives I take too long to disembark from the train and the doors close on my arm. I try to push the doors back but they don't move. I panic. My mind floods with hysteria. So this is it, all this travelling and I'm going to die on a train in Brazil. A young guy reaches over and casually pushes the doors open. Suddenly feeling free, I step back and the train departs. Breathless, I stay on the platform for a few moments. After gaining my composure I reflect on the incident—about how calm the young guy had been in saving me. How effortless it was for him, as if second nature.

At the Australian embassy, I quickly realise obtaining a proper passport will not be easy. First, my birth certificate has to be sent from Australia, then I have to find a lawyer, doctor or judge and convince them to sign a form to say they've known me for ten years. Then I have to find another two forms of ID and pay $200.

It's too much hard work. Besides, I only have 800 bucks left and don't want $200 to go on a passport. I tell the embassy I'm going to fly back to Australia. (But secretly decide to take my chances in Hawaii.)

In the afternoon I take a bus to Ubatuba, a town three hours north of São Paulo, which is the venue for the surfing contest. After 20 minutes of scattered Portuguese with the locals, I discover that there's only one hostel which is located about 5 kilometres out of town. A taxi driver takes me out there. The hostel looks like an abandoned farmhouse.

'Hostel aqui?' I ask the taxi driver, as we pull up beside it.

'Um momento,' he replies and runs through the pouring rain, then raps on the door.

Lights come on in the house.

'Se,' he yells back, 'que isso.' (This is it.)

I grab my backpack, run through the rain and into the house.

The hostel is managed by a lady with a friendly face who speaks little English. Inside, it smells like mothballs and is completely empty, so I have my pick of two rooms. I have a shower and listen to the rain, which has not stopped since I left São Paulo, pelt down on the tin roof. Having not seen any surf shops in the town earlier, I wonder if I'm even in the right place.

'Onde esta praia?' I ask the lady, after I get out of the shower and change. (Where is the beach?)

She takes me to the entrance of the house and points up at a map.

'Aqui,' she says, running a finger along the coast.

I do the maths and discover I'm still 30 kilometres from the contest site.

The next morning I wake to discover the rain has broken and the sun beats down on the house with intensity. Outside the grass is wet and smells dewy. The lady wakes, says 'Bom dia' (Good morning) and then makes me a delicious breakfast of fresh mango, pawpaw, yoghurt and hot chocolate.

I book out of the hostel and walk into town. After half an hour of confused conversations with friendly locals, I catch a bus heading towards the competition site.

'Isso e prior,' the bus driver tells me (This is the beach), and pulls the bus to the kerb of the road. I thank him and depart the bus but do not feel convinced.

I'm in the valley of a tropical rainforest. There are tall trees and shrubs and green mountains on either side. Although it's one of the most beautiful areas I've seen, it isn't a beach. On a hunch, I walk down a gravel track for about 20 minutes and then come to a little store that sells fruit and groceries. I buy an apple and orange juice and a man behind the counter informs me that the beach is only 20 minutes further along the track.

By the time I reach the beach, my backpack feels heavy across my shoulders and sweat is trickling down my forehead. The competition site is only a five-minute walk further along the beach. The whole area is in, as usual, a buzz of activity.

'Excuse me,' I say to a man working on the site. 'Surf competition aqui?'

He walks off and comes back moments later with another man.

'My name is Zacou,' the man says. 'How can I help?'

'I'm in the surf competition and was wondering if you know a place to stay and also, where to get a surfboard.'

Zacou steps back and laughs. He is stocky and short and has an earnest face. The laugh is more a natural reaction than an attempt to ridicule. I suddenly realise that the situation is actually quite funny—a professional surfer without a surfboard.

People swarm around us. A man who looks to be in his forties speaks to Zacou. Although they converse in rapid Portuguese, I can make out a few words and it seems like the man is offering a room to rent. Sure enough, Zacou turns to me and says: 'You can stay at this man's house. If you need a surfboard, come and see me tomorrow. You will always be able to find me. I'm the lifeguard for the competition and will be here for the rest of the week.'

I thank Zacou and walk with my newly acquired friend along the beach until we reach a small estuary. Although words will not do it justice, I'll attempt to describe its beauty. It's actually a small river that stops 50 metres from the beach, creating a patch of sand between the river and the breaking waves. I stand for a moment and sear the sight into my memory; the stunning contrast of the dark forest, golden beach, shiny river and turquoise ocean.

I follow the man across the estuary. It only gets waist deep and I hold my backpack over my head as we wade across it. We go onto a little track that winds through the forest and takes us out into a clearing. Here, there are muddy tracks and dishevelled homes. Eventually we arrive at the man's house which, although small, is clean and well-kept. My room is to the side of the house. Inside there is a bathroom and a double bed, which is covered in plastic wrapping—as if it has recently been bought.

I thank the man, have a shower and then join him in the main house. Any attempts I make to work out the price of the room are waved off—he tells me he'll work it out later. We watch the Brazilian news on television, which is much the same as Australian news but in a different language, and then he disappears. He comes back to the house 20 minutes later with a crooked grin.

'The girls, they will come,' he says.

'Girls, what girls?'

'The girls who live close. They want to fuck you.'

The word seems vulgar and out of character. He only speaks a little English and I wonder how he'd learnt it. The girls arrive ten minutes later. They are young and pretty but barely hide an inner toughness. They introduce themselves as Camilla and Ebony. I can tell they are survivors and feel nervous around them. As we watch TV, they smoke and ask me questions in Portuguese. I have the impression they thought I'd have the pro surfer look, and don't seem too excited about how I've stacked up. They leave an hour later and I go to bed.

Just before dropping to sleep, I hear my landlord on a phone call. From the little Portuguese I pick up, I can tell he is talking about me. Something doesn't feel right. I decide to leave first thing in the morning.

The next morning I wake early, grab my backpack, leave €20 under a rock on the cupboard and sneak off.

At the competition site, I see Zacou and ask if he knows of another place to stay.

'No problem,' he replies with a smile, 'you can stay with me.'

We work out a rate for the week ($100 Aussie) and he drives me to his house. His house is beautiful. It's located a few kilometres from the beach on top of a mountain ridge surrounded by thick rainforest. The house has two storeys. There is a large wraparound veranda on the second storey that offers an amazing view of the coast.

Zacou offers me a beer and we spend an hour chatting. He was a professional surfer in the mid 1980s, and has travelled to all corners of the globe. Having lived for a few years in Hawaii, he speaks fluent English. I sit back on the veranda, listen to his stories, look over the forest to the coast and feel relaxed and happy that I've met him.

Zacou wakes me early in the morning and drives us down to the competition site. He seems to know everybody, from bright-eyed young kids to old ladies, and proudly introduces me as an Australian surfer. As a local will tell me later, 'Zacou is like the town mayor.'

In the afternoon I see, casually leaning against a steel railing at the contest site, an incredibly good looking person. From the moment I set my eyes on Jaymes Triglone

I feel unexplainably drawn towards him. I guess most people are. If I, as a heterosexual male, can't resist talking to him, then how can a full-blooded woman? Jaymes Triglone is tall, has blond hair, square shoulders, brown skin and piercing blue eyes. Triglone is an Australian pro surfer who, if clean-shaven, would look like a movie star but his rough blond beard gives him the appearance of a hardened adventurer, as if he's just come back from a hiking expedition in the Himalayas.

We talk for a while about the competition and I find out he's due to surf in the heat after mine. While we talk, Camilla and Ebony, the girls I met two nights ago, suddenly appear. They're mesmerised by Triglone and attempt to start a conversation with him. Of course, he doesn't understand a word and I find myself being the translator.

'They like you,' I tell him. 'They want you to come with them.'

We follow the girls around to the estuary where I see Alex, the young Hawaiian who'd beaten me in the contest in Portugal, with a friend.

'What's up bro?' he asks. 'Who are the girls?'

I introduce the young Hawaiians to Camilla and Ebony. Before crossing the estuary, Triglone turns back to the beach.

'I'm going for a quick surf, be back in 20 minutes,' he says, and takes off his shirt.

The Brazilian girls are already impressed but after the

shirtless manoeuvre, their admiration seems to ascend to another level.

'Onde ele vai?' they ask me. (Where is he going?)

I tell them he'll be coming back and they breathe a sigh of relief. Meanwhile the two young Hawaiians strike up a conversation with the girls and once again I'm the translator. I don't mind. I look around at the beautiful estuary and the sun setting over the beach and the whole situation feels surreal.

Triglone appears 20 minutes later and a man paddles us across the estuary on a raft to an eco-resort, where the Hawaiians are staying. The Hawaiians, who are young enough to remind me of my little brother, invite us back to their unit. It's clear they like the girls but their hopes are dashed when Triglone produces a didgeridoo.

Didgeridoos are traditional Aboriginal musical instruments usually made from a hollow tree branch, but Triglone has made his didge in the Canary Islands from a cardboard tube and masking tape. This guy can't be serious, I think to myself, as he prepares to play. Surprisingly, he gets a good sound from it, not dissimilar to a real didge. As the noise reverberates around the room, I watch the girls' eyes glaze over.

Moments later we're kicked out of the unit by two security guards, who hear the sounds of the didgeridoo and discover that, apart from the Hawaiians, we are not paying guests at the lodge.

I say goodbye to Triglone and, on the walk back to

Zacou's house, spot Davi with a carload of Brazilians. They're staying in a house not far away and invite me back. On the veranda of their house, we drink some beers and I tell Davi about being without a board. He offers to lend me his board for my heat tomorrow.

'Are you sure?'

'Yeah, no problem man,' he says. 'I'll just grab it off you later.'

I thank him. Being his only board, I know it's a generous offer.

The next morning I catch a lift down to the contest site with Zacou. Once again, I won't be favoured by the conditions; the waves are 2 feet and crumbly. Surfing on Davi's board with hoards of pros, I get in a quick practice surf and, of course, barely catch a wave.

At the check-in area I discover the worst—I'm up against three Brazilians. In these conditions I know they surf better than anyone and will be hard to beat. I don't recognise any of the Brazilian surfers but we exchange smiles on the water edge before our heat starts and wish each other luck.

Davi's 6' 3" square-tail paddles well, and I make my way quickly through the choppy surf. Once out the back, I sit to the side of the others and wait to hear the buzzer that will start our heat. Before the buzzer, I find myself in the perfect position for two waves but I'm forced to drift over them. Typically, after the buzzer, the waves are sparse. After a few minutes of no waves, the Brazilians become restless and paddle quickly towards the beach, searching for the smaller inside waves, but I stay further out, deciding to take a chance and wait for something bigger. The other competitors ride the small waves well and quickly rack up scores between 4 and 7.

My chance comes halfway through the heat. A decent-looking wave peaks before me and I take off and do a good turn but then get bogged down on a cutback. When the wave ends I paddle back out quickly and wait for another, but the ocean goes flat. The scores come through from the judges. With a minute to go, I need a 7 to make it through. With 15 seconds remaining, a left peaks up in front of me and I take off and make a good backhand snap, then race for the next section, but the wave dies and I only manage a small floater before it fades out.

The buzzer sounds. I know I haven't scored a 7 and stay in the ocean for a while, pondering what went wrong. My score comes through as a 6. It's my highest ride on the WQS but it won't be enough. Jaymes Triglone paddles past me for the next heat.

'Don't worry about it,' he says, as if reading my mind.

At the contest area, I hand in my contest vest and then find Davi at the contest site and give him back his board.

'Hey Sully, I saw your last wave, it was good,' Davi says, slapping me on the back. 'You know you should have not have waited so long out the back bro, that was the problem.'

'Yeah I know,' I reply. 'Thanks for the board, it went well.'

I walk along the beach, then sit for a few moments watching Triglone's heat. He's a naturally talented surfer but is not helped by catching the wrong waves and being underscored. He finishes third.

I catch up with him later on the beach. He looks dejected, and wants my opinion on what went wrong. I tell him I thought he was harshly scored by the judges. We sit in a beachside café, eating muesli and yoghurt. He talks about his travels; he's just come from the contests in the Canary Islands.

'The worst thing is having to go back to Australia and tell family and friends about being knocked out in the first round here,' he says, munching muesli.

'Do you have any other creative outlets apart from surfing?' I ask.

'Yeah.'

'What are they?'

'I'll show ya,' he says, and I follow him across the beach.

We wade across the estuary to a small hut that he's booked for the competition. Inside it's clustered with surfboards and wetsuits. He reaches into a bag and pulls out a tattered green book.

'I'm going to read you some of this, don't judge me.'

He reads from the book. It's a combination of abstract observations, drawings and free-verse poetry. The poetry is actually quite good and he reads it fast, like a rap song. Having only met Triglone yesterday, I realise that it's courageous of him to share his poetry with me.

'What do the other surfers think of your writing?' I ask when he's finished.

'I haven't shown them, they think I'm a tripper,' he laughs. 'I just showed you because you seem different.'

I spend the morning talking with him. He shows me how to play the didgeridoo and tells me about a six-month course he has recently completed in outback Australia on Aboriginal appreciation.

'I have a plan,' he states boldly. 'I want to start a group of writers and photographers and surfers. Imagine what we can achieve together. You want in?'

I sit back and realise that, at the least expected moment, I've stumbled upon something real. If he has a plan, I'll be in it—I'll happily travel anywhere with him. It's amazing to think how, in the vacuum of pro surfer coolness, someone like Jaymes Triglone exists. In a subculture of trendy shoes, how can he prefer to walk barefoot across muddy tracks to 'feel closer to the earth'? Among a group of hungry single-minded aspirators, how can he spend six months in remote Australia to better understand Aborigines? As the whole world leans towards instant gratification, how can he prefer to build a fire and cook on it because it feels like the 'right thing to do'?

As far as interesting characters on the tour go, I did not expect anyone to trump Josh Lewan. As usual, I'm wrong. I've misjudged Triglone. Last night, with the didgeridoo and starry-eyed girls, I thought it was all an act. Now I know the truth. He is real. His marketing potential is scary—if only the surf companies knew. He's an authentic, good-looking, rugged professional surfer who plays the didgeridoo. He actually is the cut-out image of what Hollywood spends millions on trying to define.

At night, looking for action, I walk through the village with Triglone. With his straggly hair and poncho he looks like a flashback from the 1960s. It's a clear night and we walk along the dirt roads. We stop at a café and order a sandwich. The café is really just an open tin shed. There's a bar, a few tables and chairs, and a group of young teenagers playing pool.

The teenagers invite us over for a game. The pool table is old and scratched and has a horrible lean but no one cares. The kids are wide-eyed and ask us where we're from and then Triglone gets out the didge and impresses everyone.

The sound of Triglone's didgeridoo acts as a beacon. Suddenly, people surround us. One of these, a guy with long black hair who looks about our age, invites us back to his house. His house is only a few hundred metres from the café. Inside, it's bare apart from a couch and a chair. The floor of the house is concrete, there's no carpet or tiles and there's no door, just a sheet covering the doorway, but the man is not embarrassed and enthusiastically motions us onto the couch. In the corner of the house is an old guitar. He picks it up and plays it loosely and Triglone joins in with the didge.

For an hour, people come in and out of the house and listen to the music. The long-haired man introduces himself as Fabio. He cannot speak English and I translate his Portuguese to Triglone. Pretty soon we're all laughing at the funny sound of the homemade didgeridoo. The night is lucid and rolls on like it's going to last forever. Eventually, we say goodbye to Fabio and I walk back to Zacou's house and drop to sleep feeling happy.

The finals of the surfing contest are held in a 3-foot swell. Unfortunately, Davi is knocked out before the money rounds and Mick Campbell has withdrawn because of a knee injury. It's a shame for Mick, as he's still chasing ratings points and a shame for me, as I was looking forward to seeing him surf. Adriano de Souza performs well in the first semi-final but suffers from bad wave selection, something that seems to plague him often. Troy Brooks, once again, looks like the favourite. With his combination of power carves and radical airs, he cruises through to the final.

The other finalist is a Brazilian called Renan Rocha. Zacou had told me about Rocha the previous day. He's a local from a poor family and Zacou had taught him to surf. Having been raised by a family where any trip to the beach is a rare privilege, it's incredible that Rocha even made it to the pro level.

Although it's plain to see that Brooks is a better surfer in the final, somehow he fails to catch the right waves and Rocha wins the event. When it's finished the Brazilians go mad. I watch Zacou tow Rocha in to the beach on the jet ski. At the awards ceremony, Zacou presents the trophy to Rocha with a tear trickling down his face.

After the presentations I meet a charismatic surf photographer called Ernie. Ernie, having been raised in America, is quirky and funny and speaks with a clear American accent. It feels good to bounce off his jokes and he invites me to a party organised by the surf brand Onbongo—the main sponsor of the event. After walking across the beach, he finds a raft hidden in the scrub and we paddle across the estuary with the sun setting and the taste of Brazilian beer in my mouth and the joy of Brazilian life on my brain. We walk across a track and then come to a clearing and a little house where Ernie is staying. Inside, he shows me his surf photography.

'You know man,' he says, sipping a beer, 'I can't quite figure you out. I bet you must rip.'

'I hold my own,' I tell him, knowing, of course, that I'm a complete fraud.

'I'm doing a photo shoot tomorrow at a wave down the coast, you should come bro.'

'Sounds good,' I reply, reasoning that he'll have forgotten the invitation by tomorrow.

We go to the Onbongo party and then to a bigger party in the town. This party is held in a two-storey castle with an open roof. It's an amazing venue. By wearing my competitor's pass, I'm allowed to drink free beer and feel pretty good swooning with the attractive Brazilian girls under the stars. Later, when a DJ is in full swing with upbeat house music, Dayyan Neve approaches me.

'Hey mate, no matter what happens tonight we'll get good reception,' he says, and points to a massive antenna above the castle.

I laugh. During the day, Neve, after being knocked out of the competition, had worn a yellow G-string on the beach. As usual, I now realise I've misjudged him from the initial impression he'd made on me by wearing the fighter pilot glasses in Durban. At contest sites around the world I've mistaken his humour for arrogance. He's actually a funny larrikin.

All night I watch the pros being picked off by Brazilian girls. At the end of the night I meet a girl called Alana and, of course, try all my drunken schmoozer moves, this time in Portuguese. I kiss her as the sun rises over the castle and it feels too good. But suddenly a shocking feeling hits me. It's a feeling strong enough to penetrate skin, and it thuds hard into my solar plexus and crawls into my brain. The feeling is not made up of guilt or anxiety, or hurt, or pain, or worry. It's pure fear.

The feeling is this: One day blood will not pump through my veins; air will not fill my lungs. I will not be able to stand with a girl on the balcony of an old castle in Brazil and see the sun rise. I will not see anything at all. There will be no consciousness. There will still be incredible sun rises. The morning light will still bounce from tree leaves in Brazil. Waves will still form on the outer reefs of Indonesian islands. The full moon will still hang low and shiny above the headland of Jefferys Bay. But I will not see it. Because my existence on this planet is brief. My life is not forever. And this majestic living breathing earth doesn't really care about the life of me.

I know, as I watch this sun rise, that I will never live with four walls and a backyard. Life insurance policies will not be signed. Possessions will not be accumulated. I must go, go, go. I must continue travelling, discovering, living. I must keep meeting the crazy cats. Life is too short for boundaries.

I walk from the party in the direction of Zacou's house, my mind still buzzing with these thoughts. Along the way I bump into Jaymes Triglone and Ebony.

'Hey man, you going to Hawaii?' I ask.

'Nah, I'm staying with Ebony for a week and then going back to Australia.'

He says goodbye and I watch them walk off. He doesn't know a word of Portuguese and she doesn't know a word of English but it doesn't seem to matter.

At Zacou's house, I pack up my gear and, with the sun now well up in the sky, make my way to the airport.

Re: Hawaiian Event Entry Deadlines
From: Brodie
Sent: Thursday, 12 October 2006 9:34:55 AM

Dear Competitors,

Just a reminder that Monday 16th October is the entry deadline for the 6 star Van's Hawaiian Pro and the 6 star OP Pro Hawaii Women's WQS. Thursday 26th October the 6 star O'Neill World Cup.

All those wanting to enter these events must do so before 5PM on the deadline days.

Entries can be done online or by contacting ASP Australasia. The events are filling up fast so all late entries will be placed on alternate lists.

Kind regards,

BJC
ASP Australasia Administration
Surfing Australia

Hawaii, October

Getting into Hawaii on an emergency passport will not be simple. Even leaving Brazil may not be without hazards considering I've overstayed my visa. My visa is a single piece of paper with an eight-day exemption. After being allowed to enter Brazil, I was told to keep the visa by customs officers at São Paulo Airport, so that it could be stamped when leaving. Knowing that the piece of paper will confirm that I've overstayed, I decide to ditch it before arriving at the airport and take my chances.

When I attempt to check onto my flight to Hawaii at the airport in São Paulo, a customs guard casually flicks through the pages of my passport.

'Where is your visa?'

'Visa?' I say, as if it's the strangest word in the universe. 'What visa?'

'Wait here,' he says, and directs me away from the queue.

I sense deja vu. I really don't want to go back to the holding cell.

He returns with a supervisor who asks the same question and I give the same 'Visa, what visa?' reply. The two men begin a lively argument. From what I can make out, the young customs officer wants to question me further but the older one, who looks tired and fatherly, hands back the passport and lets me walk on.

When arriving in Hawaii, in an ironic twist, I'm actually helped by the new security measures. There is a new rule that all foreigners entering America must have their eyes scanned and fingerprints taken. Knowing that my emergency passport is invalid for the six months required, I deliberately bump the eye scanner and knock the fingerprint pad every time the customs officer looks down at my passport. The guard eventually becomes frustrated and after I complete the eye test and fingerprint, he stamps my passport and lets me move on.

I walk through the airport foyer feeling pleased with my dodgy antics. Later, I discover it was more luck than skill. A Brazilian surfer I'd met in France, Jihad Khodr, was sent back to Brazil a few years ago because the customs officer, in light of the terrorist attacks, didn't like his name. When entering Hawaii, Khodr was ranked just outside the top 15 and only needed a good result in the final two WQS events to qualify for the WCT.

Outside, my shirt sticks to my skin in the humidity and every passing car seems to be a bulky four-wheel drive.

I catch a bus from a bus stand near the airport.

'How far to the North Shore?' I ask the driver.

'About 40 miles, but it'll take a few hours by bus.'

With the sun already low in the sky, I realise it will be dark by the time I arrive. I consider staying in Waikiki for the night which, having spoken to other travellers, I know is only a few miles from the airport and offers a thriving night-life. Sensibility returns; now is not the time to be distracted.

'Can I please have a ticket to the North Shore?' I ask the driver.

'Sure buddy,' he replies with a smile. 'You have to ride this bus for about 20 miles and then get off and catch another one. I'll tell you when.'

I thank him and ride the bus for an hour. Once I'm on the second bus, a guy with a military outfit walks up the aisle and slumps beside me, exuding the body language of someone in a bad mood.

'What's wrong?' I ask.

It's not my place to pry but I feel talkative.

'Just got kicked off the last bus for swearing,' he explains.

'That sucks.'

'Yeah, son of a bitch bus driver left me high and dry, and I only got six hours till they want me back at base.'

I stare at the man in wonder. Since spending time in California five years ago, it has never ceased to amaze me how forthcoming Americans are.

Slowly, people disembark from the bus and by the time

we reach the North Shore, I'm the only person on board. I ask the bus diver if he knows any cheap places to stay and he drops me outside the North Shore Backpackers.

At the reception area, a guy with a stubble-covered chin and southern American accent confirms the worst: 'Sorry buddy, it's full for the next few days.'

I tell him that I'm happy to sleep anywhere.

'Well, normally you could sleep on a mattress in the lounge but two guys are already doing that. I really don't have a place for ya.'

As I'm halfway out the door, he says: 'Listen, I'm not meant to be telling ya this as it's our competition, but there's a place with cheap accommodation a few hundred metres down called Shark's Cove Rentals.'

I thank him and walk to Shark's Cove Rentals. On the front veranda, I knock on the door but there's no answer. Hearing noise from the back of the house, I go around to a fence and call out to people who are cooking meat on a barbecue.

Their demeanour is welcoming and they tell me I have to call John, the owner, to enquire about a room. They write down John's number and then lend me their phone. I speak with John. In that typical American way, he's quickly hospitable and enthusiastic over the phone. He offers a private room for $80 a night. Although it's a quarter of what I have left, I feel too tired to argue and accept. I enter the room, turn on the air-conditioner and barely have enough energy to take off my clothes before dropping to sleep.

I wake feeling refreshed in the morning. While talking to the other tenants, I discover it's only a five-minute walk west to Waimea Bay or a 15-minute walk east to Pipe. The revelation startles me. The two most famous waves in the world are only a 20-minute walk apart and I'm smack-bang in the middle of them.

With newfound enthusiasm, I take off in search of Pipe. Along the way I pass old people enjoying a brisk morning walk. Each person catches my eye and greets me with a cheery 'Good morning'. Having read numerous articles in surfing magazines about brutal localism in Hawaii, the friendliness of people who live here, especially those who don't surf, surprises me.

I walk onto the beach. The sand feels soft between my feet. I see a lifeguard in those famous red boardshorts and it feels like I'm in a movie. He is a young Hawaiian with a thick build and olive skin. I say hello to him.

'Hey guy, how are you today?' he replies.

'Where do you reckon is the best place for a wave?' I ask, stoked on the conversation.

'There's not much goin' on at the moment, you might wanna try Log Cabins.'

'Where's Pipeline?' I ask.

'It's about another ten minutes down the beach.'

'Thanks.'

I keep walking until I reach Pipe. It's barely breaking and there are only a handful of bodyboarders surfing it but my excitement remains undiminished. I sit on the beach

and let the sand run through my fingers. My whole life
has led up to this moment. I've been dreaming about this
place for 20 years and here I am, sitting straight in front of
the most famous wave on the planet. I sit on the beach and
stare out at the waves slowly spilling only a few metres from
the beach. It's hard to imagine this as the bone-crunching
wave I've seen in videos and magazines. I sit back and
imagine the waves are huge.

Eventually, I walk back to Shark's Cove and meet John. He
looks about 45, has a pleasant manner but is hard to budge
on price negotiations for accommodation. After continual
haggling, I get him down to $20 a night to sleep in a spare
tent in his backyard.

'If you need work, you should check the noticeboard at
Foodland,' he advises me.

I walk to Foodland. All that's required is a quick skirt
through the aisles of the supermarket to confirm that I'm
in the heart of the surfing universe. Men have square jaws,
loose T-shirts and shoulders that look strong enough to
propel them to another island. The girls are tanned and
healthy.

I buy two bananas and an orange juice and then scope
for employment on the noticeboard. A labourer is required
to help with a lawnmowing round. I call the number. A
man with a friendly gravelly voice answers and I try my best
to charm him. He agrees to let me start tomorrow.

My new boss, Norm, picks me up from Foodland at seven o'clock the next morning. He's about 50, speaks with an earnest grin and his white beard gives him the appearance of the colonel from Kentucky Fried Chicken. My duties are pretty simple—just raking up leaves and lawnmowing. Wanting to make a good impression, I work hard and he appreciates the effort, giving me an extra $5 at the end of the day.

After work I find an internet café and write an email to Bobby to ask if he's in Hawaii.

I only have $300 left but being in Hawaii without a surfboard feels ridiculous so I go searching for a second-hand board in the afternoon. There's a surf shop only 50 metres from Shark's Cove. It has a small veranda stocked full of surfboards. Inside, the relaxed vibe of the shop strikes me as being familiar. A guy with curly blond hair, who looks about 19, walks up to greet me. His name is Paul. He expresses himself slowly, and his speech is full of the kind of lingo that sounds like the caricature of a Californian surfer.

'Where you at?' he says.

'Pardon?'

'Where are you stayin' on the North Shore?'

'Just down the road at the Shark's Cove Rentals.'

'No way, I actually helped build those apartments with John. I still work for him every now and then. What kind of board are you looking for?'

'I was thinking a 6' 4".'

'You'll probably need something bigger for out here,' he says with a smile, and takes me outside to the back of the shop, which is crammed with big-wave guns.

I ask him about the price of the boards. The majority are $300–500 and are beyond my budget. As I walk out of the shop, I see a photo hanging on the wall of Liam McNamara riding a tube at Pipe.

'I met that guy in Spain,' I tell Paul.

'You met Liam, no way, he actually owns this shop. He's coming here in ten minutes. You should hang around. He'll probably give you a discount if he knows ya.'

'Thanks, but I've gotta go,' I reply, feeling a sense of dread.

The tactic has backfired. I don't feel like seeing Liam — what if he discovers that I didn't make the speech in Spain?

Back at the Shark's Cove, a group of rowdy men are playing poker in the outdoor area.

'Hey buddy, it's only $5 if you want in,' a guy informs me.

The guy's name is Maddi and he introduces me to his friend Eric; they are both Americans. I say hello and sit beside them then meet the other two players, who are Swiss marathon runners training for the next Olympics. I throw down $5 and we play poker, drink beer, eat potato chips and exchange jokes for the rest of the night.

The next morning I drive around with Norm raking leaves and lawnmowing. Some of the homes are built right on the beach and their backyards actually spill onto the sand. At one house, which offers a beautiful view of the surf spot Rocky Point, I get a glimpse of the surfers. Norm catches me looking wistfully at the waves and says: 'Hey buddy, let's take a break.'

He pulls up two chairs and offers a bottle of water.

'Do you surf?' I ask, as we watch the surfers.

'Nah, gave up a few years ago. It's a young kid's game. I was out there in the BC era.'

'BC?'

'Before cords.'

I laugh at the joke.

We spend a few hours on the lawns and then he drops me outside Foodland and I feel pretty content with myself; another 50 bucks stuffed in my pocket. On the walk back to Shark's Cove, Paul calls out from the veranda of the surf shop.

'Hey bro, come here, Liam's in.'

I walk slowly over, hoping Liam doesn't quiz me about the speech I was supposed to make in Spain.

Liam greets me with enthusiasm: 'Hey buddy, I recognise ya from Spain.'

Just when I think he's going to ask me about the speech, he says: 'Paul tells me you're looking for a board, you might be in luck. Pancho has just dropped in a few.'

He looks me up and down. 'You look like a big guy. How much do you weigh?'

'About 90 kilos.'

'So that's about 200 pounds. I think that's the same as Pancho.'

Liam pulls one of Pancho's old boards from the rack.

It's a nice-looking round-tail 6' 5". Pancho Sullivan is a Hawaiian pro currently ranked about 20th on the WCT. He's always been a favourite surfer of mine and it feels strange to check out his boards.

'How much do you want for that one?' I ask Liam, pointing at the 6' 5".

'$350 should see ya right.'

Considering it's Pancho's old board and in good condition, it's a bargain, but I only have a few hundred dollars left.

'Any chance you might sell it a bit cheaper?'

'You're a nice guy. I might be able to get it down to 300.'

I wonder why Liam's being so friendly to me. I still feel like a rat for not making the speech in Spain. I tell him I'll try and rustle up as much money as possible.

Back at Shark's Cove, there's another energetic poker game in progress and I throw down $5 on the table. Later, a group of us walk down to the beach and share a carton of beer; sipping the cans with the rumble of the waves crashing down on the shore beside us.

The next morning after breakfast, I catch a bus to Haleiwa to look for a surfboard. With my last $200, I buy a nice-looking 6' 2" square-tail that has been shaped by a local Hawaiian board maker called Eric Arakawa. The board is probably not going to have enough foam in it for the big swells but I hope it can at least surf well in the smaller conditions.

In the afternoon, Paul arrives at Shark's Cove looking

for John Junior (the landlord's son) to go surfing, and I manage to catch a lift with them down the coast to a surf spot called Lonnies. Lonnies is a powerful right that breaks a few hundred metres offshore and reminds me of the waves in Margaret River.

I paddle out on my 6' 2" feeling that the board is too small for the conditions. There are about 30 surfers in the line-up, ranging in age from 18 to 40. Some of the surfers are pros and all are competent. The waves, which I hear other surfers call 8 feet, surge through the ocean quickly and I feel under-gunned on my new board, but it's my first surf in solid waves since South Africa and I'm happy to be out. I sneak a few of the smaller ones off the pack and have fun racing the long walls. The Arakawa board goes surprisingly well in the thick waves and I feel happy with my decision to buy it. I stay out until after dark and then hitchhike with Paul back to Shark's Cove.

At Shark's Cove I discover that Maddi and Eric, having flown back to the mainland, have been replaced by four loud young Aussies. The Aussies look about 19, are tanned and muscly, and have a tendency to walk around shirtless. Two of them have mohawks and three have tattoos. There's something about them that feels comfortable — they remind me of my youth. During the poker game they laugh, punch and make constant threats to shave off each other's eyebrows. I can see where this is leading, of course — it'll only be a matter of time before the pranks start heading my way.

Later, the Aussies find out about a party a few blocks away. The party is held in a two-storey house packed with surfers and beautiful girls. We rock up unannounced and with little alcohol, and try unsuccessfully to swindle both the girls and the booze. Ironically, the Swiss marathon runners are polite to everyone, have their own beer and end up being punched out by a local.

The last three contests of the year are referred to as the Triple Crown. They are held at the three name breaks on the North Shore—Haleiwa, Sunset and Pipe—and are the most prestigious events for professional surfers to win. The last competition of the Triple Crown, at Pipe, is a WCT event but the first two, at Sunset and Haleiwa, are 6-star WQS competitions and offer the surfers on the WQS a final chance to finish inside the top 15 and qualify.

The contests at Sunset and Haleiwa are run differently to normal WQS events. To make way for Hawaiian wild cards and WCT surfers, only the top 100 ranked surfers on the WQS are allowed to enter. Realistically, it's anyone with a shot at qualifying. This means that Josh Lewan, Bobby Morris, Dean Randazzo, Davi de Jesus and myself do not get a berth. While travelling, I have heard some surfers complain about the Hawaiian system—that it's too exclusive, and favours Hawaiians and surfers on the WCT rather than those who have toiled hard on the WQS throughout the year.

The Haleiwa event runs for a week in a patchy swell. Every day after work I catch a bus down to the competition site to check it out. During the heats, the WCT surfers show their experience and knock out most of the other competitors. The contest is won by Taj Burrow.

At the end of the contest, I catch a bus back to the Shark's Cove to discover two new people in the rooms—a middle-aged hyperactive punk rocker called Bill, and a tall blonde girl from the Czech Republic called Maria, who is quick-witted and nicknames the young Aussies 'dingoes', because they are constantly falling over each other. Bill and Maria are both outgoing types and gel well with the drinking culture.

During the week I surf up and down the coast with Bill. Apart from surfing Pipe on a small day, I try to avoid surfing the famous breaks on the North Shore. I prefer being away from the pros and find the atmosphere too intense on the 4-kilometre stretch between Sunset and Log Cabins. Anyway, there are good waves to find away from the name spots and Bill has a new four-wheel drive, and seems happy to drive around and explore the other waves.

On the day the Americans call Thanksgiving, I wander down to Pipe. The swell has picked up and looks dangerous. Spectators, lifeguards and cameramen line the beach, and a few crazy nuts are out surfing. After watching Pipe for a while, I walk a few hundred metres down the beach to a break that's even more treacherous, called Off the Wall.

'How big do ya reckon it is out there?' I ask a cameraman on the beach.

'10 to 12,' he replies, barely taking his eyes from the lens.

'Who's out there?'

He turns to me and smiles. 'Just KP and some of his lunatic Aussie mates.'

KP is short for Kieren Perrow. He's a professional surfer that I've occasionally seen at other WQS contests. Because he's sponsored by Rip Curl and surfs well, I initially judged him as being image-conscious and egotistical. Throughout the year, however, I'm proved wrong.

In Ubatuba, Perrow was knocked out before the finals of the contest. At the time, because he was ranked outside the top 15 and desperately needed points, I expected him to come to the beach in a foul mood and was surprised when he'd handed back his rash vest to the beach marshal with a smile. At airports, he has always met my eyes and said hello. Perrow's low-key personality is in stark contrast to most of the surfers on the WQS. On the land he's quiet. In the water he's fearless.

Off the Wall breaks quickly over a shallow shelf. The wave is thick, powerful, hollow and will often shut down. Surfing in these conditions is critical. Come off, and you're likely to hit the reef. I sit beside the cameraman on the sand and watch, mesmerised. The huge waves only break about 80 metres from the shore and it's amazingly theatrical to watch the surfers ride them. I flirt with the idea of running back and grabbing my 6' 2" Arakawa square-tail but know that the waves are out of my league. The surfers paddle into the waves without hesitation. Their reflexes are lightning-quick. Maybe it's a talent you're born with.

In the afternoon I hitchhike up the hill from Shark's Cove to Pupukea, where Norm's friends are hosting a Thanksgiving dinner. It's an amazing feast of pumpkin pie, salad and turkey. The hosts are a friendly old couple who dress me in a Hawaiian shirt and happily tell me about the origins of Thanksgiving. (It's a celebration from when the pilgrims of America had saved enough food to ensure they would survive the winter.)

Later, back at the tent, there are eggs and bananas in my bed. I know it's a prank from the Aussies and decide not to react. Lately, the dingoes have been content to cajole me into some kind of strange alpha-male love/hate relationship. After defeating them in an arm wrestle a few days ago, they've become more brazen and make constant threats about shaving my eyebrows. And another night before an approaching storm, they had me convinced that they'd punctured my tent with a knife and I spent half an hour searching for holes.

Also, our drinking is getting out of control. Yesterday John, under the impression that I'm the most responsible, gave me the role of nightwatchman. What he doesn't understand is that I secretly like the dingoes' rebellious nature. The truth is the dingoes are nuts. One day they invite me to bodysurf a shore break next to Log Cabins.

The waves are 8 feet at Log Cabins and 6 feet on the shore break. I decline to enter the water. For two hours I watch the Aussies being continually pole-axed into the sand and coming up laughing.

According to the locals, it has been a bad winter for surf but the swell picks up for the Sunset contest. The Sunset competition is the last WQS event for the year. I work with Norm during the mornings and watch the competition in the afternoons. The waves are clean and powerful for the week and once again the WCT surfers dominate the event. Joel Parkinson wins. The WQS surfers perform better this time against the WCT guys, but still not many WQS surfers make it into the finals. Although Mick Campbell is knocked out early, his work has already been done earlier in the year by winning the two 6-star French contests. Mick finishes the year second on the WQS rankings, only a few hundred points behind Jeremy Flores. It's an incredible achievement. He'll now head back to Australia, all set to tackle the top 45 on the dream tour next year.

A few days after the Sunset competition I walk to an internet café and receive an email from Bobby that says he's already left Hawaii.

In the afternoon, I meet a photographer called Geoff at Shark's Cove, who tells me he is keen to take shots of Waimea Bay. Waimea, the most famous big-wave break in Hawaii and possibly the world, only breaks when the swell is at least 10 feet. I jump in his car and we drive down to Waimea, pull up on the side of the road overlooking the bay, and watch the swells come rolling through. It's a small day by Waimea standards but the surfers still look like ants when dropping down the face of the waves.

'Why don't you go out there?' Geoff asks me.

'I don't have a board big enough.'

'What about that big red board back at Shark's Cove?'

The red board is Norm's. After a lawnmowing job a few days ago, he'd told me nostalgic stories about surfing Waimea as a teenager, then took me back to his shed and dusted off the big red board.

'Here ya go,' he said, handing the board over with a smile. 'If ya ever get the balls to surf Waimea, this will get ya into them.'

I have no excuse. Geoff drives me back to Shark's Cove, I tie the big red board onto the roof of his car, and then we drive back to Waimea. Geoff wishes me luck and I run down to the sand with the board. There are not many people on the beach. I see a massive set of waves breaking on the outside. I consider turning around but then hear words of encouragement from Geoff: 'Go get 'em bro.'

With a pounding heart and tasting fear, I brace the surf, make my way quickly through the shore break, and then start paddling for the outside reef. The old red board paddles easily through the water, and it doesn't take long to propel myself 500 metres out and be sitting alongside the other surfers.

The surfers in the line-up range in age between 18 and 50. They all look incredibly fit and are riding boards more than 8 feet in length. In the surf, they casually sit up on their boards, cracking jokes and laughing with each other, but I'm careful not to be lulled into a false sense of security. I've experienced this kind of banter by the surfers of Margaret River in big waves. The bigger the waves, the more relaxed some people act to offset fear. When a set of waves does eventually make its way towards the impact zone, I paddle frantically for the channel.

The first wave is caught by the guy furthest out. Although the wave is big and moving quickly, he gets into it early and makes the drop comfortably. The second wave goes through unridden then three guys turn around and share the third wave, and I watch in wonder as they drop down the face of it.

Then I turn and see them 100 metres down the line, shouting and joking as they pull off the shoulder. They happily chat with each other on the paddle back out and the thought hits me that big-wave surfers are a strange breed. How can they be so relaxed surfing waves of such consequence?

Inspired by their casual demeanour, I make my way closer to the peak. Another set of waves marches through from the deep water and hits the reef. Two surfers in front of me paddle for the first wave of the set, but are 5 metres too far out and cannot get into it. There is a guy on the inside of me who has the right of way but, possibly reasoning that the other surfers are going, he commits himself to drift over it. I suddenly realise I'm in the perfect position for the wave. I have half a second to decide on paddling for it. This is it, now or never. I turn around and paddle and in that half a second—when I feel the thing surge beneath me and look down the steep, fast-moving wall of water, when I sense I'm going to catch the ride of my life or be smashed to within having an inch of air left in my lungs—I know this journey has not been about competing against other surfers.

It's not about sunglasses, or clothes, or casual conversations, or feeling like I'm a part of something. It's not about the ratings, or impressing girls, or being ashamed to carry a board down the beach because it doesn't have any sponsorship stickers.

When it's all stripped back, it's just about me and the wave.

I put my head down and paddle hard and feel the water draining quickly back up the face of the wave, holding me in the lip. I look down. I'm not going to make it. I consider jumping out and diving down the face of the wave to steer clear of my board, knowing the last thing I want in condensed ocean pressure is to be hit in the head by fibreglass. At the last moment I give one extra paddle and jump to my feet as the spray gusts into my face, momentarily blinding me. When I open my eyes I'm racing rapidly down it.

I make it to the bottom of the wave, crouch low on

the board and bottom-turn towards the shoulder. Hearing the wave thump behind me and sensing that a mountain of whitewater is about to mow me down, I crouch lower. Then the whitewater crashes around me and I can feel myself losing balance. I hold on for as long as possible. Just as I think I'm about to fall, the wave dies and I'm pushed quickly out into the channel. I give a quiet howl, jump onto my stomach on the board and begin the paddle back out to the other surfers. It's the best feeling in the world.

Pipe, October

O n the eve of the Pipe contest, the young Aussies find out about a party at the Volcom house. Having read about the Volcom house in surfing magazines, I know its reputation. The house, owned by the surf brand Volcom, is situated on the beach at Pipe. The only people game enough to visit the house are surfers sponsored by Volcom, hot girls, famous pros and heavy locals. Even the dingoes baulk at the prospect of showing up at the party unannounced.

'So, you guys gonna come with me?' I ask them.

'Nah.'

'Why not?'

''Cos we don't have an invite, idiot.'

I tell them I'm going. I really don't know the reason behind these reckless pursuits but it feels like a challenge. They reply with laughter and make bets on how long I'll stay in one piece. Then they drive me down the road and drop me on the Volcom house doorstep, shouting encouragement from the safety of their car.

Telling myself I'm an idiot, I walk around an alleyway to the back of the house. It's too late to chicken out. Fortunately, the only people on the back veranda of the house are a bunch of kids, who look about 16, playing foosball—that game where you control the little figurines and try to get the soccer ball into the goals. The kids are decked out in Volcom gear and are obviously young guns being groomed as future pros.

I introduce myself and ask if I can play. They're all polite and happily accept my offer, so I take up a position on the table and start playing the game with them. I guess they've assumed I know someone and that I'm supposed to be here.

During the night surfers file into the house. There seems to be an abundance of free alcohol at the party and no restrictions on who can drink it. Before leaving, one of the young surfers hands me a half-full bottle of vodka.

'It's all yours, I wanna get a surf in the morning without a hangover,' he tells me.

I thank him and store the bottle in the pocket of my shorts.

Later I meet Sarah, a student at the university in Honolulu. She asks who I'm sponsored by and I respond vaguely, then suggest we go for a walk down to the beach. We walk hand-in-hand along the beach. It's a clear starry night.

'Let's go up here,' I suggest, pointing to the podium where the winner of the Pipe contest will be announced.

We kiss on the podium underneath the full moon. I look around and can just make out the whitewater breaking at Pipe in the darkness and wonder if I'm becoming addicted to this feeling—the feeling of being a complete fraud. I remove the bottle of vodka from my shorts and have a long swig.

The rest of the night is a blur.

I wake up in a strange house on a strange bed. My hangover feels powerful enough. Sarah has disappeared. A girl I don't recognise, wearing pink pyjamas and talking in a high-pitched voice, comes into the room and offers me water. I thank her, drink the water and leave the room. Outside, I see two student types.

'How far are we from the North Shore?' I ask them.

'About 40 miles,' the short guy answers.

I rub my head.

'We're going to drive there to check out the surf contest at Pipe if you wanna come,' he offers.

We ride back to the North Shore in a jeep. The students are called Dan and Ross and, in that typical American way, don't find it unusual that I'm a complete stranger who has accosted them on the street.

It's midday by the time we reach Pipe and the contest is halfway through round 1. I feel a light breeze on my back as we make our way onto the beach. Although the waves are big, they don't break far from the shore and it feels like the beach, which is packed with people, is a natural amphitheatre.

In the surf, the waves are 8 feet and perfect and the WCT surfers ride them beautifully. Nobody baulks, but the best performers are the Aussies and the Hawaiians. I spend the day on the beach, feeling privileged to watch the incredible surfing display, and slowly feel the alcohol drain from my body with my sweat.

Norm picks me up early the next morning. I'd prefer to spend the day watching the Pipe contest but am stone broke — not in a position to refuse a day's work. I rake leaves in a backyard only a few hundred metres from Pipe and watch spectators stream past. As I'm about to throw a bundle of mouldy pine cones into a bin, Nathan Hedge walks past me with a surfboard tucked under his arm.

'G'day mate,' he says with a smile, and motions towards the rotten pine cones, 'those look yummy.'

I stand motionless, stunned. Since France, I've been trying to avoid Hedge. In an hour he'll surf a heat at Pipe that'll determine his future on the WCT, yet he still has the presence of mind to be friendly to me.

I've been wrong about Lewan, Neve, Perrow, Triglone, Fahrenfort (who, since I met in Newquay, has always said hello to me around contest sites), and now, I realise, I've been wrong about Nathan Hedge. My initial judgement of the pros was based on my own insecurities — of being wary of anyone who was a better surfer than me. Learning that behind the vests and confidence and new boards and infallible professional surfing system, the surfers are mostly nice people, is a revelation that I'll carry with me for the rest of my life.

Andy Irons wins the Pipe contest. Unfortunately, Hedge gets knocked out early and is relegated off the WCT. He'll be back toiling on the WQS next year.

On my final morning in Hawaii, I wake the same way I have been for the past week—feeling for my eyebrows. I share the flight back to Australia with a hoard of pros. Layne Beachley is two rows in front of me and Joel Parkinson two rows behind.

At baggage collection in the airport at the Gold Coast, my Eric Arakawa 6' 2" square-tail, which is covered by an old 1970s-style board bag that I found discarded underneath the house at Shark's Cove, is, of course, the first off the carousel. I feel embarrassed picking up the tattered board bag beside the collection of brand new shiny ones. I guess I always will.

I arrive on the Gold Coast instead of Perth because my parents are on a holiday here for a week, and have sent an email inviting me to join them. When I walk through the arrivals area, however, I can't see them anywhere. I find them a few hundred metres away—they've gone to the wrong terminal.

They say hello and take the board bag from my shoulders.

'Where are all the pro surfers?' my dad asks with excitement.

'They went the other way,' I reply.

It feels like the right end to the journey.

2006 WQS Top Qualifiers

Competitor	Position	Points accrued
Flores, Jeremy FRA	1	11255
Campbell, Michael AUS	2	11190
Basnett, Ricky ZAF	3	10210
Bryson, Royden ZAF	4	9755
Neve, Dayyan AUS	5	9535
Brooks, Troy AUS	6	9515
Padaratz, Neco BRA	7	9454
Kerr, Josh AUS	8	9420
Dunn, Ben AUS	9	9275
Patacchia, Fredrick (jnr) HAW	10	9135
Miranda, Bernardo BRA	11	9121
Kling, Gabe USA	12	9045
Ribas, Victor BRA	13	8970
Neves, Leonardo BRA	14	8790
Otton, Kai AUS	15	8545
***	***	***
Davi de Jesus	108	3608
Bobby Morris	122	3324
Josh Lewan	202	2762
Jaymes Triglone	311	1984
Sullivan McLeod	567	486

Epilogue

Well well well, three holes full of water.

I met a girl at a comedy club once who insisted that I start my routine with that joke. I then dutifully told the joke to an eager crowd and did not receive a single laugh. To that girl, if you happen to be reading this, I forgive you.

Well well well, two years have passed since my hectic year on the WQS—plenty enough time for reflection. My year on the surfing tour sometimes feels like a surreal dream so I'm glad to have this book to remind me that it happened.

I'm writing this on a lazy Sunday afternoon from a musky-smelling pine desk inside the tree house in Margaret River. Down at the point today, the waves are 6 feet and powerful and offer good shape to the eight surfers riding them but I've decided to show some discipline and decline the surf. Considering that my year on the surfing tour is being turned into a book, I think it's a good idea to let you (dear reader) know what happened to a few of those zany characters I met on my journey.

But first, to clear up a few points. Having my gear stolen on the beach in France is true. At the time I'd been keeping a rough journal of the trip but gave up recording information after the journal, along with everything else, disappeared on that fateful night in the coastal village of Biscarrosse-plage. Although *Tunnel Vision* is written in present tense (apart from the first chapter), the entire book was not actually started until after I finished the surfing tour. Basically, the book was written from memory. Therefore, as much as I tried to get the right feeling or mood of events that transpired, it is not always exactly accurate.

Also, sometimes I deliberately exaggerated parts of the book. There is more to Australian Rules football, for example, than 18 men beating the crap out of each other under the guise of following a football but I wrote like this for comic effect and I hope that you'll allow me some poetic licence.

There are some parts of my year on the WQS that I have deliberately omitted from the book. The reason for this is to protect people from things that I think they would not want recorded in public. I apologise for not revealing everything but believe it is important to keep some stories to myself. Anyway, in the main, *Tunnel Vision* covers all the best bits of my year on the surfing tour.

And so to the surfers: Bobby Morris visited me last year for the 2007 Margaret River Masters. We had fun surfing up and down the coast for a week but unfortunately he was knocked out in the first round of the contest. Coincidently, Kieren Perrow won the Margaret River event that year and qualified for the WCT. I haven't seen much of Bobby in the past year but occasionally watch him online competing at WQS events in America.

Davi de Jesus unfortunately suffered a back injury at the end of the 2006, which kept him out of the contests for a year. I occasionally keep in touch with him and received an email a few weeks ago; his back has recovered and he's considering returning to the WQS.

I bumped into Josh Lewan a few months ago at the surf contest in Margaret River. He still wore his trademark smile but no diamond earring. Although still competing in WQS events in Australia, these days Josh is more focused on music. At the contest area, he had a copy of his latest songs and handed over his headphones to let me listen. In the afternoon he was meant to sing his songs live but, unhappy with the acoustics on stage, did not perform. Regardless, it seems that his music career is on the brink of taking off. Last year in *Cleo* magazine, he was voted in the top 50 coolest people in Australia.

While watching the Margaret River contest online last year, I heard Jaymes Triglone being mentioned as one of the surfers in the next heat. I only live a few kilometres from the contest site, so I jumped in my car and headed down there, hoping to catch up. Unfortunately, the road was jammed that day with people driving to the contest and I had to settle for a carpark 500 metres from the surf. By the time I reached the contest site, Triglone's heat had finished. He'd come third. I searched the contest area but failed to spot him and walked away disappointed, resolving that his mysterious enigma status was firmly intact.

Then a few weeks ago, I googled his name on a whim and discovered that he's an international model. Apparently, a European scout spotted him in Sydney, and then immediately offered him a position as the face of Armani. Weeks later Jaymes was strutting his stuff on the catwalks of Milan. Online, I read a newspaper article where Triglone's mum found it hilarious that Jaymes was selected as an international model: 'He wore the same pair of shorts for years … he basically lives in a wetsuit, shorts and nothing on his feet.'

Remembering back to that night in Brazil, where Triglone was casually strolling barefoot through the muddy tracks of Ubatuba, wearing an old poncho and hitching a didgeridoo across his shoulders, I also find it hard to imagine him in designer suits.

It seems Triglone has been busy since the modelling work. As well as appearing as an actor on the ABC series *Blue Water High* and in a movie called *Newcastle*, he was also nearly arrested in Japan when protesting with a group of high-profile surfers and actors against the killing of dolphins. But for me, I will always remember him as he was 20 minutes after losing his heat in Ubatuba—inside an old hut reading free-verse poetry from a tattered green book.

Nathan Hedge was relegated off the WCT in 2006 and so far has failed to requalify. Currently, he's outside the top 15 on the WQS but has a shot at qualifying this year (2008). Troy Brooks lost his spot on the WCT in 2007. He is also back on the WQS attempting to qualify. Dayyan Neve qualified for the WCT in 2006 and has performed well. Currently he's ranked inside the top 30. The ever-smiling Adriano de Souza has made a great start to the 2008 World Championship Tour; currently he is sitting in 4th place.

As mentioned in this book, Michael Campbell qualified for the WCT in 2006, and has also performed well, ending the 2007 year ranked 18th. In 2008 he has had mixed results, but will hopefully finish with a burst and requalify.

Dean Randazzo continued recovering well from his cancer. Very recently, he received a stem cell transplant from his brother Joe. Reading his last diary entry from a website (www.deanrandazzocancerfoundation.org) he set up with friends, he says he 'can't wait to get back in some surf'.

I didn't spend much time writing about Dean in this book, mainly because I only saw him in two contests, but find him a truly inspiring person. The cancer foundation he helped to start is a non-profit organisation that has already raised more than $100 000 for people battling cancer and

I strongly recommend anyone reading this to log on, check it out and, if you can afford to, give generously.

Jason Carstens, my manic boss in Melbourne, no longer works for the Comic's Lounge. He has started a training school for puppies. He still lives in Melbourne, performs stand-up comedy, and regularly goes to Australian Rules football games to berate the players and coaches.

Pizza Shop dropped around to our place a few weeks ago. He no longer drinks much or takes antidepressants and has an easygoing girlfriend. Together, they plan on travelling around Australia for a year and then becoming highbrow art dealers. I must admit I'm impressed with the new Pizza Shop, but very occasionally I catch a glimpse of something in his eye—that familiar spark—and know the good ol' Pizza Shop is not far away.

As for me, I'm still surfing most days and chasing the crazy cats.

Peace and Love
Sullivan

Surf lingo explained

360: When you rotate your board 360 degrees and then continue surfing.

8 feet: A wave measurement. Usually when surfers say the waves are 8 feet, they are referring to the size of the back of the wave. The actual face of the wave is usually a lot higher. Works the same way with 1 foot, 2 feet, etc.

Air: A surfing manoeuvre where your board leaves the wave and then lands. A lot of speed is needed to perform this manoeuvre.

Air reverse: A type of air where the board spins and lands backwards on the wave. You can then keep turning the board to complete the 360.

ASP: Association of Surfing Professionals. The body that governs professional surfing.

Beach break: A wave that breaks on sand.

Board bag: A bag designed to carry surfboards.

Bodysurf: To swim down the face of a wave and ride it (without your surfboard).

Bottom-turn: The first turn at the bottom of a wave, after making the drop, which will propel you back towards the face of the wave.

Breaking zone: The place in the ocean where the waves break (surfers mostly refer to this as the impact zone).

Carve: A fluid and powerful turn on the wave.

Channel: An area of deep water. Sometimes water will flow back out to sea through the channel, and waves will not often break there.

Charger: Someone who pushes themselves in the surf, exuding the courage to ride big waves, i.e. 'That guy on that last wave is a charger.'

Check-in: The area at the contest site where competitors register for the event.

Chop: Bumps on the waves created by strong winds, which makes surfing more difficult.

Closing out: When a wave shuts down or dumps, meaning you cannot ride the wave left or right but have to go straight.

Contest vest: The vest competitors wear (usually red, yellow, white and blue) which distinguishes them in the surf to judges.

Cutback: A 180-degree turn that's done by digging your rail into the wave. This then propels you back towards the whitewater.

Dig-a-rail: When the rail of your board gets pushed into the wave accidentally, causing you to lose momentum or fall from your board.

Ding: A crack or dent in the fibreglass on the surface of the board.

Ding-repairer: A person responsible for fixing dings.

Drop: The initial slide down the face of the wave after springing from your stomach to your feet on your surfboard.

Drop-in: Taking off on a wave that is already being ridden by another surfer, or to take off on a wave when another surfer is closer to the breaking part of the wave and already has the right of way. Dropping-in is considered a sin in surfing.

Duck-dive: A technique used by surfers (by pushing the nose of your board down with your knee) to dive underneath an impending wave and avoid being smashed.

Face: The wall of moving water that the surfer rides.

Fat: Waves that have little power or shape.

Fibreglass: Strands of finely woven glass used as the sealant on surfboards.

Fins: The devices on the bottom of a surfboard which help to control movement.

Flat: When the waves are not breaking or very small.

Flicking out: Manoeuvre used to kick your board off the back of the wave.

Floater: A manoeuvre where you ride across the top part of the wave (lip) before dropping back down to the base of the wave.

Foam: The whitewater that forms from a broken wave.

Goofy-footer: Surfer who uses their right foot on the surfboard as their front foot.

Grommet: A young surfer.

Grovel: To surf in small waves.

Hassle: Using tactics to harass the other surfers in a competition.

Heat: The period of time that surfers in a competition are judged. Heats on the WQS typically go for 20 minutes, with your top two rides counting.

Impact zone: The part of the ocean where the waves break.

Kook: Not a very good surfer, or an inexperienced surfer.

Leash: The flexible cord that is tied from your board to your ankle, which stops the board being washed away in the waves.

Left-hander: A wave that breaks from right to left allowing the surfer to go left (the surfer will be going right if you're watching from the beach).

Leg rope: Same meaning as leash.

Line-up: Place where the surfers sit waiting for waves, which is slightly further out than where the waves are breaking.

Lip: The curling top part of the wave.

Log Cabins: The name of a surf break on the North Shore of Hawaii, between Pipe and Waimea.

Malibu: A long board that is bigger than the standard surfboard and has a rounded nose.

Natural foot: Surfer who uses their left foot as their leading foot. (Means the same as regular foot.)

New school: Current or contemporary surfers who perform the latest progressive manoeuvres when surfing.

Nose: The top part of a surfboard.

Off the Wall: Famous surf break on the North Shore of Hawaii between Pipe and Log Cabins.

Old school: Older style of surfer, or person who performs the older type of manoeuvres.

Out the back: When you refer to a position that is far out to sea.

Over the falls: To get sucked over with the lip of the wave, causing a wipe-out.

Pack: The group of surfers that are sitting out the back waiting for the waves.

Peak: An approaching wave which peaks up and sometimes gives the surfer the option of going left or right.

Pipe: Probably the most famous wave in the world, a very hollow left-hander on the North Shore of Hawaii.

Pitched: When you are thrown from the top of the waves, resulting in a wipe-out.

Pros: Professional surfers. (Surfers who make a living from surfing.)

Quiver: A collection of surfboards in different sizes, which are suitable for different surf conditions.

Radical: An extreme manoeuvre. Something unexpected, usually has a positive meaning, i.e. 'That floater was radical.'

Rail: The fibreglass edge of the surfboard. While riding a wave, you can lean into the rail to turn your surfboard.

Recreational surfers: The surfers who are not in the competition, but usually surfing beside the competition zone.

Reef break: A wave that breaks above a reef. Usually these waves break further out than beach breaks and have more power.

Re-entry: When you ride up to the top of the wave (lip) and then turn back down to re-enter the wave.

Right-hander: A wave that breaks from left to right, allowing the surfer to ride the wave to the right (the surfer will be going left if you're watching from the beach).

Rip: A current which flows beside the break. Rip can also mean a person who surfs well, i.e. 'The kid on that wave rips.'

Rip Curl: A well-known surf brand.

Round-tail: A surfboard that has a rounded curve on the bottom of the board.

Sandbank: Where sand has built up on a beach break, causing the waves to break.

Secret spot: A surf break that surfers are trying to keep secret from other surfers.

Set: A group of approaching waves. Usually there are three or four waves in a set.

Shaper: A person who shapes the foam that creates a surfboard.

Shore break: A wave that dumps on the shore.

Shoulder: The fading face of the wave, where you can flick out.

Shut-down: Where the wave closes out on the surfer. This can also be when you're inside the tube but fail to escape before the wave shuts down.

Single fin: A board with only one fin. Usually these have been shaped in the 1970s or earlier, before the invention of the thruster.

Snap: A fast turn, usually in the critical part of the wave.

Square-tail: A surfboard with a square edge at the bottom of the board.

Sucky: Description of a wave that jacks up and breaks quickly. These waves are difficult to surf and usually break in shallow water.

Superman air: A manoeuvre where you hold the board with your arms and throw out your legs.

Swell: The moving waves before they reach the sand or reef and break.

Tail: The bottom part of a surfboard.

Tail slide: A surfing manoeuvre where you slide the tail of your board out on the wave.

Thruster: The three fins on the bottom of a board which help the surfer to change direction and maintain control on a wave. Simon Anderson was credited with the invention of the thrusters in the 1980s. Before thrusters, surfers rode twin fins and single-fin boards.

Tombstoning: When you're held down deep underwater by a large wave and the pressure of your weight causes the board to rise vertically from the surface. Tombstoning usually only happens in big powerful surf.

Tube: The gap between the pitching lip of the wave and the wave face. Experienced surfers can ride inside the tube and come out.

Tunnel: Same as tube; also the gap betwen the pitching lip and face of the wave that experienced surfers can ride.

Under-gunned: When the boards a surfer owns are too small for the waves.

Waimea Bay: The famous big-wave surfing break on the North Shore of Hawaii.

Wall: The moving face of water that surfers ride.

Wax: The substance that is rubbed into the deck of the surfboard to stop you falling off.

WCT: World Championship Tour.

Wedge: The part of the wave that jacks up quickly and forms a wedge shape before it breaks.

Wetsuit: Made from rubbery polystyrene; this is worn for warmth in the surf.

Whitewater: The white foam created from a breaking wave.

Wipe-out: Falling from your surfboard into the wave.

WQS: World Qualifying Series.

Acknowledgements

This book would not be possible without the help of a group of fine women from Allen and Unwin. Luckily for me, the initial manuscript was detected from other unsolicited submissions (in what publishers refer to as the slush pile) by a very industrious person called Jennifer Castles. Thank you for noticing my submission Jennifer. The copyediting was done by the very insightful Susin Chow. Thank you Susin. Advice and ideas were freely given by the talented Elissa Baillie. Thank you Elissa. For the cover, thank you Josh. Last but definitely not least, thank you so much to the very accommodating and passionate commissioning editor Andrea McNamara, who bought me lunch twice, had to put up with my squabbling over small things throughout the process, and still stuck her neck out and thought I was worth publishing.

For initial encouragement and support with earlier writing, thank you to Malcolm Edwards in England,

Marit Bodtker in Norway, and my dad, Keith McLeod, in Margaret River. Also thanks to Chris McLeod who gave feedback about the inner workings of the publishing world.

I know this is a long list, but to the people who have been kind to me, not so much in the literary world but when they've come across my down-and-out dishevelled self in different parts of the globe, thank you to Eddie Kommers, George Wren, Jantien Schipperijn, Andrew Strahan, Joel Andrew, Shaun McCurry, Paul Waring, Ryan Neilson, Acky, Anette Larsen, Chad Bonciani, Benedikt and Sevi Clasen, Dan Carney, Joakim Hoiseth, Dave Grant, Leonieke Toolen, Brendan Windle, Tim Brett, Nathan Baber, Daz man, BJ Hookem, Jonathan Boyle, Stoffa, Mijke Hertzberger, Nicole Marentette, Geoff Stainton, Michael Howell, Stephanie Wood, Martin and Anders at Vestvingin, Janneke Van Wingerden, Luke Williams, Renate Harford, Luke Hutchings, Magnus Winther, and the ever-smiling geezer Richard Massey.

To my close-knit relatives all over Australia: my amazing nana in Exmouth; Roo, Rack, Auntie Lo and family at Warroora Station; Uncle Lyall, Auntie Gem and family in Perth; Uncle Neil, Auntie Coz and family in Margaret River; Steve and Karen in Adelaide; Lee in Margaret River; Mary, Richard and family in Mandurah; Perry and family in Albany; and Geoff and Julia in Perth, thank you for your endless support. Special thanks to my own family (Dad, Mum, Jack, Ash and Connor) for always giving encouragement and putting up with me.

Finally to all the surfers and interesting characters I met on the tour, especially Jason Carstens, Harry Keeffe, Pizza Shop, Kristin Camp, Bobby Morris, Josh Lewan, Michael Campbell, Zecao Renno, Dean Randazzo, Davi de Jesus and Jaymes Triglone, thank you for letting me tag along ... it was an incredible adventure.